MINI

ENCYCLOPEDIA

OCEANS

MINI

ENCYCLOPEDIA

OCEANS

Miles
Kelly

First published as *Ocean* in 2009 by Miles Kelly Publishing Ltd
Harding's Barn, Bardfield End Green, Thaxted, Essex, CM6 3PX, UK

Copyright © Miles Kelly Publishing Ltd 2009

This edition printed 05/14

LOT#:
2 4 6 8 10 9 7 5 3 1

Publishing Director Belinda Gallagher
Creative Director Jo Cowan
Series and Volume Designer Helen Bracey
Cover Designer Jo Cowan
Image Manager Lorraine King
Picture Researchers Jennifer Cozens, Ned Miles
Indexer Eleanor Holme
Production Manager Elizabeth Collins
Reprographics Stephan Davis, Jennifer Cozens, Anthony Cambray
Assets Lorraine King
Consultant Clint Twist

ISBN: 978-1-4351-5642-5

Printed in China

British Library Cataloging-in-Publication Data
A catalog record for this book is available from the British Library

Made with paper from a sustainable forest

www.mileskelly.net
info@mileskelly.net

Contents

Ocean features

Ocean life

Exploration and travel

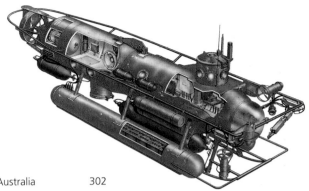

Ocean features

A planet is born

★ **It is believed** that about 15 billion years ago a huge explosion, called the big bang, led to the formation of the universe.

★ **The first galaxies**, including our own Milky Way, started to evolve about a billion years after the big bang. Clouds of dust and gases came together to form stars.

★ **Until about five billion years ago**, the solar system was a huge cloud of dust and gases drifting through the Milky Way and containing rocky and icy particles.

★ **The cloud** became a swirling hot disk called a solar nebula. The gases and dust began to squeeze together until the center became hotter and hotter and eventually exploded, creating the sun.

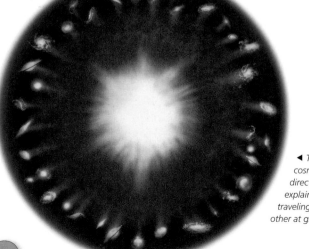

◄ The big bang threw cosmic matter in all directions. This theory explains why galaxies are traveling away from each other at great speeds.

- **The icy particles** near the sun melted, but the dust particles around it started to clump together to form small rock nuggets. Over millions of years, these nuggets grew into huge boulders called planetesimals.

DID YOU KNOW?
According to a theory, nearly 4.5 billion years ago an object as big as Mars collided with Earth. It scattered a lot of debris in space. The debris gathered to form our moon.

- **These planetesimals** began to collide into each other. They soon built up into the four rocky inner planets—Mercury, Venus, Earth, and Mars.

- **Far away** from the sun's heat, icy particles and leftover gases combined to form the outer planets—Jupiter, Saturn, Uranus, and Neptune. Pluto, Charon, and other dwarf planets were formed even farther away from the sun.

- **Unlike the inner planets,** the atmospheres of the outer planets contain huge amounts of gases such as hydrogen, helium, ammonia, methane, and carbon monoxide.

- **These outer planets** are collectively called the gas giants because they are primarily made up of gas, unlike the inner planets that are composed of rock. These planets are also bigger and colder.

- **It is widely believed** that Jupiter, the largest planet, caused the destruction of the planetesimals around it. Due to Jupiter's strong gravitational pull, these planetesimals crashed into one another, leaving behind a belt of rock fragments called asteroids.

The blue planet

★ **Earth** is the only planet in the solar system with enough oxygen and water to support life. However, it was not always so. At first Earth had no oxygen or atmosphere. Only traces of hydrogen and helium were present.

★ **When it first formed,** Earth was continuously hit by rocks and other materials from space. These collisions generated immense heat, causing rocks to melt.

★ **At the same time,** radioactive elements on Earth released a lot of heat, causing heavier elements such as iron and nickel to sink deep into the center of the planet to form its core. Lighter elements such as silicon floated to the surface.

★ **The layer** surrounding the core is called the mantle, which is in a partially molten state. The mantle comprises the bulk of Earth's weight and volume.

DID YOU KNOW?
Acids in the rainwater corroded the rocks on Earth's surface. Chemicals in these rocks were carried into the oceans. Among these chemicals were certain salts that made the ocean water salty.

★ **About four billion years ago,** Earth's surface cooled and solidified to form the topmost layer, called the crust. The crust was broken into several rock fragments, called tectonic plates, that floated on the mantle.

★ **These plates** moved past each other, often colliding and causing friction. These collisions built up pressure beneath the crust, leading to volcanic eruptions that caused cracks on the planet's surface.

▼ *Volcanoes continuously erupted, covering the surface of the primeval Earth with oceans of lava, making it unfit for life.*

Gases, such as hydrogen and nitrogen, and water vapor burst through the cracks in the crust. These constant eruptions slowly led to the formation of the atmosphere.

Water vapor condensed to form clouds that enveloped the planet and eventually brought rain. However, Earth's surface was so hot that the rainwater evaporated immediately.

As the rains continued, Earth started to cool and the volcanic activity decreased. Water poured down for thousands of years to fill up huge pits and form oceans.

The rain also formed smaller bodies of water such as rivers and lakes. At high altitudes, the water froze and fell as snow. The snow melted and flowed down mountains as streams and rivers.

Oceans of the world

⭐ **Oceans cover** almost 140 million square miles of Earth's surface. Although there is only one ocean that covers the world, it has been divided into four ocean basins. A fifth ocean, the Antarctic Ocean, also called the Southern Ocean, was recently added to this list.

⭐ **The four basins** are the Pacific, Atlantic, Indian, and Arctic oceans. The Arctic Ocean surrounds the North Pole and is largely frozen.

⭐ **The Antarctic Ocean** is actually formed by the southern extensions of the Pacific, Atlantic, and Indian oceans. Hence this ocean was, for a long time, not considered as a separate entity.

⭐ **The international dispute** regarding the status of the Antarctic Ocean continued until the year 2000. The International Hydrographic Organization has since recognized the waters surrounding Antarctica as the fifth ocean and named it the Southern Ocean.

⭐ **The Pacific Ocean** is the largest of all oceans. At 64 million square miles, it is twice the size of the Atlantic Ocean. The Pacific Ocean's average depth is more than 13,000 feet, making it the world's deepest ocean.

⭐ **This ocean** gets its name from the Spanish word *pacifico*, which means "peaceful." During his voyage around the world, Portuguese explorer Ferdinand Magellan found the Pacific to be calm and hence gave the ocean its name.

⭐ **The second-largest** ocean is the Atlantic Ocean, at 32 million square miles. It is also the stormies, and has a mid-ocean ridge that runs through its entire length.

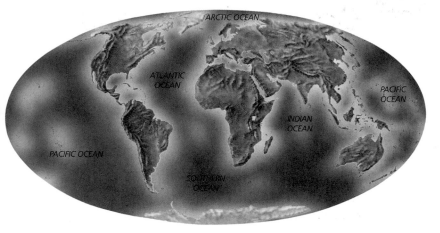

▲ The world's oceans cover most of our planet. Each
ocean is made up of smaller bodies of water called seas.

✦ **The Atlantic Ocean** contains some of the most important
seas and other features. These include the Baltic Sea, Black Sea,
Caribbean Sea, Mediterranean Sea, Gulf of Mexico, Labrador Sea,
Denmark Strait, and Norwegian Sea.

✦ **The Indian Ocean** has a total area of over 28 million square miles.
It is bounded by the three continents of Asia, Africa, and Oceania.
Some of the earliest known civilizations, such as the Mesopotamian,
Egyptian, and Indus Valley civilizations, developed near the ocean.

✦ **At 5.4 million square miles**, the Arctic Ocean is the smallest
among the world's oceans. It is also the shallowest. The deepest
point in the Arctic Ocean is only 17,880 feet—not even half as
deep as the deepest point of the Pacific Ocean.

Causing waves

⭐ **Oceans are never** completely at rest. They are rocked by several kinds of movements, including waves, currents, and tides.

⭐ **Most movements** in the oceans, such as waves and surface currents, are caused by wind. Waves are created by winds blowing over the surface of the oceans. The stronger the wind, the larger the waves.

At high tide, the water level rises.

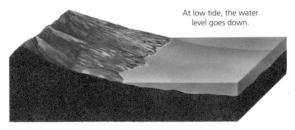

At low tide, the water level goes down.

▲ High tide happens on those parts of the planet that are closest to and farthest away from the moon. As Earth turns, approximately six hours later the water subsides. This is called low tide.

★ **The water in a wave moves** in circles and not forward as it may appear. As a wave nears land, it slows down because of the shallower seabed. The top part of the wave carries on and crashes on the shore as a breaker.

★ **Waves differ** in shape and size. A steep, choppy wave is one that has just been formed near the coast, while the slow, steady ones are those that originated far out in the ocean.

★ **The regular rise and fall** of the oceans are called tides. They are caused by the gravitational pull of the sun and the moon. Since the moon is closer to Earth, its effect is felt more.

★ **High tide** is the period of high water level; the period of low water level is known as low tide.

★ **An ocean current** is a mass of water moving continuously in one direction. Surface currents are caused by winds and the rotation of Earth, while differences in temperature and salt content are responsible for underwater currents.

★ **Most ocean currents** flow in large loops called gyres, which spin clockwise in the Northern Hemisphere and counterclockwise in the Southern Hemisphere. This is due to Earth's rotation and is called the Coriolis effect.

★ **When the sun, moon, and Earth** are in a straight line, their combined gravities cause unusually high tides, called spring tides. This alignment of the three happens during full moon and new moon. Smaller tides, called neap tides, occur at other times when the moon is at a right angle to the sun and Earth.

The angry oceans

⭐ **The oceans**, which are a source of invaluable resources, can also wreak havoc in the form of tsunamis, whirlpools, and hurricanes.

⭐ **There are times when** a series of massive waves are generated in the oceans by certain natural disturbances. These waves, called tsunamis, lash against the shore with such great force that they cause a lot of damage.

⭐ **Tsunamis** are most often created by earthquakes. They can also be generated by landslides and undersea volcanic eruptions, and are often incorrectly referred to as tidal waves. In 2004 a massive tsunami, caused by an earthquake in the Indian Ocean, resulted in the deaths of around 300,000 people.

⭐ **Most tsunamis** originate along a volcanic and earthquake-prone zone known as the Ring of Fire, around the Pacific Ocean. *Tsunami* is a Japanese word meaning "harbor wave."

⭐ **Hurricanes** are violent tropical cyclones arising in tropical or subtropical waters. Hurricanes of the northwest Pacific Ocean are called typhoons.

⭐ **The strongest and most dangerous hurricanes** are classified as category 5. These hurricanes are rare and the wind speed exceeds 155 mph.

★ **A whirlpool** is created when opposing currents or tides meet in the ocean. The uneven ocean floor makes the water swirl in with great force. Most whirlpools are not dangerous. However, some are powerful enough to destroy small boats.

★ **Moskstraumen** off the coast of Norway and Old Sow near Deer Island in Canada are two of the world's most powerful whirlpools.

★ **Another interesting oceanic phenomenon** that has a considerable effect on global weather is El Niño. It is the warming of surface waters in the eastern Pacific Ocean, near the equator.

★ **El Niño causes** an increase in rainfall across the southern states of the United States and in parts of South America. This usually leads to destructive floods in these regions. It is also believed to be responsible for drought in Africa and Australia.

◄ *Waterspouts are spiraling columns of water that can be sucked up by a tornado as it forms over the sea.*

21

Coastlines

* **A coast** is a continuous stretch of land that borders an ocean. It is made up of sand, mud, and gravel. The outline of the coast is called a coastline.

* **The features** of a coast depend on the wind, rocks, and currents in that area. Strong winds whip up equally strong waves that pound the rocks on the coastlines and erode them.

* **Hard rocks** are able to withstand the pounding of waves and erode slowly, forming headlands.

* **Wave power** is also responsible for the formation of structures such as cliffs, headlands, sea caves, sea arches, sea stacks, and beaches.

Sea stack

◀ *Waves can create amazing shapes in rock, such as pillars called sea stacks.*

Arch

★ **A cliff** is formed by the constant pounding of waves on weak spots on the rock face. At first, a tiny gap is created. This gap enlarges as the rock continues to erode, eventually causing its roof to collapse.

★ **When softer rocks** at the base of a cliff erode first, they collapse onto the shore. They break into minute fragments, eventually forming wide beaches between the existing cliff and the ocean. This saves the cliff from further erosion.

★ **Continuous erosion** leads to the creation of hollows, called sea caves, in the headlands. Sometimes waves pound the headland from either side, causing caves to form on both sides of the headland.

★ **When two back-to-back caves** meet, a sea arch is formed. The top portion of the arch links the headland to the mainland like a bridge.

★ **After years of erosion**, the sea arches cave in. This leaves only a column of rock standing independently in the sea. This is known as a sea stack.

★ **The best known** natural structure formed by the action of waves is the beach. Waves lose much of their power in shallow waters, and instead of eroding they start depositing sand and shingle, carried into the oceans by rivers, on the coast. These deposits eventually become the beach.

Sea caves

✶ **Sea caves are formed** when the force of the waves wears away rocks situated at the base of cliffs.

✶ **These rocks** are usually weak due to a fault or fracture in them. Even veinlike cracks are enough to cause rocks to crumble under continuous pounding by huge waves.

✶ **Waves penetrate** cracks in a rock and exert high pressure, forcing the rocks to crumble from within, forming small hollows.

✶ **These hollows** expand further when sand, gravel, and rocks brought by the waves start eroding the inner walls of the rocks.

✶ **Some sea caves** are submerged in water during high tide and can only be seen when the water recedes.

✶ **These caves** are a great attraction for adventurers and tourists. They can be explored in small boats or on foot when the water level is low.

✶ **Sea caves** are common on the Pacific coast of the United States and in the Greek islands. The Blue Grotto of Capri in Italy is famous for the bluish glow of its waters. This glow is caused by sunlight pouring through an underwater hole. The light shines on the water to create a brilliant blue glow.

✶ **One of the largest known sea caves** is the Painted Cave on Santa Cruz Island off California. It is nearly 1,230 feet long. The cave gets its name from the colorful patterns on the rocks.

✶ **Sea caves are full** of marine life. Sea anemones, sponges, and starfish are found in the bigger caves.

▲ Sea caves on the island of Cyprus. Caves can be of various sizes. Some may extend hundreds of feet into the rock and have more than one tunnel.

Ocean floor

⭐ **Earth's surface** is covered by the oceans and seven huge landmasses, called continents. Oceans cover about 71 percent of our planet's surface.

⭐ **At certain places** the land rises above the water to form continents and islands. The surface under the oceans is called the ocean floor.

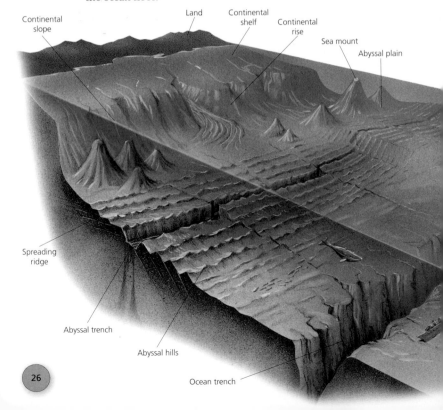

Continental slope

Land

Continental shelf

Continental rise

Sea mount

Abyssal plain

Spreading ridge

Abyssal trench

Abyssal hills

Ocean trench

🌟 **The ocean floor** is broadly divided into the continental shelf, the continental slope, and the deep ocean floor.

🌟 **The continental shelf** is an underwater extension of the coast. The rim of islands and continents gently slopes into the surrounding water to form the continental shelf.

🌟 **The average width** of the continental shelf is about 40 miles but some, such as the Siberian Shelf in the Arctic Ocean, can extend up to 900 miles.

🌟 **The continental shelf** is commercially very important. It contains large deposits of petroleum, natural gas, and minerals. This area also receives the most sunlight, and marine life thrives here.

🌟 **The continental slope** is the point where the shelf starts to plunge steeply toward the ocean floor. Here the ocean floor is marked by deep canyons.

🌟 **Below continental slopes**, sediments often collect to form gentle slopes called continental rise. The continental shelf, slope, and rise are together known as the continental margin.

🌟 **In many places** the ocean floor forms vast expanses that are flat and covered with sediment. These regions are called the abyssal plains.

🌟 **The abyssal plain** is broken by mid-ocean ridges, such as the Mid-Atlantic and the East Pacific rise, and trenches such as the Mariana Trench in the Pacific Ocean.

Volcanic island

◀ *Beneath the oceans is a landscape similar to that found on land.*

Trenches and ridges

⭐ **The ocean floor**, like land, has high mountains, deep valleys, canyons, and vast plains. The most dramatic of the ocean floor structures are the trenches, or deep valleys, and ridges, or mountain chains.

⭐ **Earth's crust** is made up of several huge, flat rock segments called tectonic plates. These plates slide and move against each other.

⭐ **The movement** of these plates is responsible for the formation of ridges and trenches.

⭐ **Ridges are formed** when two plates drift apart. Hot lava oozes out through the cracks and cools to form a ridge. A trench is formed when the heavier plate plunges beneath the lighter one.

⭐ **The Mariana Trench** is one of the deepest trenches. It is located in the Pacific Ocean, to the east of the Philippines.

⭐ **The Challenger Deep**, in the Mariana Trench, is the deepest point on Earth. At 36,197 feet, its depth is more than the height of Mount Everest.

⭐ **The mid-ocean ridge** is the longest mountain chain on Earth. It is over 30,000 miles long. The crests of these mountains lie nearly 8,200 feet below the ocean surface.

⭐ **At some places** the mid-ocean ridge is exposed above the sea level. Iceland is located on top of one such crest of the mid-Atlantic ocean ridge.

⭐ **Seamounts are** underwater volcanoes. A flat-topped seamount is known as a guyot, while those with peaks are known as seapeaks.

▼ At 1,814 feet, the CN Tower could stack inside the Challenger Deep 19 times!

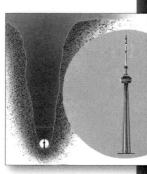

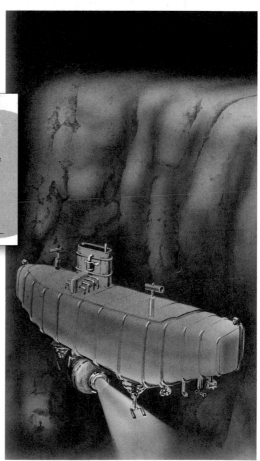

▶ On January 23, 1960, U.S. Navy Lieutenant Don Walsh and Jacques Piccard, a Swiss scientist, set a record by descending to the bottom of the Challenger Deep in the U.S. Navy submersible, Trieste.

Volcanic oceans

⭐ **Almost 90 percent** of the world's volcanic activity takes place under the ocean. Most undersea volcanoes are along the mid-ocean ridge.

⭐ **The Pacific Ocean** contains more than 80 percent of the world's active volcanoes. These volcanoes encircle the ocean along the continent margins to form the "Ring of Fire."

⭐ **Volcanoes are formed** when two tectonic plates drift apart and hot molten rock called magma oozes out. They are also formed if one plate crashes into another.

⭐ **When the lava** oozing out of an underwater volcano comes into contact with water, it solidifies quickly. This lava often forms round lumps called pillow lava. Several tiny marine organisms thrive on these lumps of lava.

⭐ **Underwater volcanic mountains** are known as seamounts. Some seamounts, called guyots, are extinct volcanoes with flat tops. Some guyots could also have been volcanic islands that were eroded with time.

⭐ **Hot springs**, or hydrothermal vents, are also found on the seafloor along the mid-ocean ridge. They are formed when water seeps into the crust as two plates pull apart. This water is heated by the magma and shoots up through cracks in the ocean floor.

DID YOU KNOW?

Mauna Kea and Mauna Loa in Hawaii are the tallest volcanic mountains on Earth. Measured from its base on the ocean floor, Mauna Kea at 32,152 feet is taller than even Mount Everest.

▲ *Hydrothermal vents are home to rattail fish and sea spiders as well as giant tube worms.*

The temperature of water in and around a vent can go up to 750°F. This water is rich in minerals and the gas hydrogen sulphide.

The scalding water mixes with the surrounding cold water to create chimneylike jets of warm water. These jets are often black because of the mineral content in the water. Hence hydrothermal vents are also called black smokers.

Hydrothermal vents were first discovered in 1977 near the Galápagos Islands along the eastern Pacific Ocean basin. Scientists traveling in the submersible *Alvin* observed these vents about 8,200 feet below the ocean's surface.

The water at the deep-ocean floor is too cold for creatures to survive, but hydrothermal vents are like underwater oases. Long tube worms and other life-forms that are not found anywhere else in the world thrive near these vents.

31

Volcanic islands

⭐ **Undersea volcanoes** often lead to the formation of volcanic islands. Some of these islands are formed around one or two volcanic vents, while others can be made up of a series of vents.

⭐ **Volcanic activity** usually occurs at the point where two tectonic plates meet or break away. Sometimes volcanoes are formed away from the plate boundaries near areas called hot spots, which are fixed points of volcanic activity located beneath the tectonic plates.

⭐ **Molten magma** from deep within the mantle forces its way through fissures in the plate and flows out to form seamounts.

⭐ **Over millions of years**, magma keeps oozing out of these seamounts, which gradually rise above the ocean surface as islands. These islands are called oceanic high islands.

⭐ **The constant movement** of tectonic plates eventually carries an island away from the hot spot, and volcanic activity ceases on that island. Meanwhile, another island is created near the hot spot. This continues until a chain of islands, such as the Hawaiian Islands, is created.

1 Molten rock breaks through Earth's crust.

* **The hot spot** in the Pacific Ocean is currently under the "Big Island" of Hawaii, which is the largest among the Hawaiian Islands.

* **The Big Island** has five volcanoes. They are Kilauea, Mauna Loa, Mauna Kea, Hualalai, and Kohala. Kilauea is the most active volcano in the region.

* **Iceland was formed** by volcano activity near the ocean ridge. It is the only part of the mid-oceanic ridge that emerges from the surface.

* **Some volcanic islands** are formed in the shape of arcs, such as the Marianas and the Aleutian Islands in the Pacific Ocean.

* **Island arcs** form when one plate slides below the other. The magma oozes out, forming volcanoes on the edge of the plate above. These volcanoes eventually emerge from the ocean surface as islands in the shape of an arc.

▼ *When volcanoes erupt under the sea, new islands may appear.*

2 As more lava is deposited on the seabed, a cone shape builds up.

3 When this breaks the water's surface, a new island appears.

Amazing corals

★ **An atoll** is a low-lying coral island consisting of a coral reef surrounding a lagoon. There are several stages in the formation of an atoll, and it could take millions of years for the island to emerge.

★ **The first stage** of atoll formation includes the creation of a coral reef around a volcanic island. Strong winds and waves slowly erode the island and it begins to sink. But the reef continues to grow upward to form a barrier reef separated from the sinking island by a lagoon—a barrier reef island.

★ **The barrier reef islands** continue to sink until the land is completely submerged. However, the reef around the island continues to grow upward to form a ring surrounding a lagoon. This is called a coral atoll.

★ **Coral atolls** are formed mostly in warm and shallow waters of the Indian and Pacific oceans. The Marshall, Tuamotu, and Kiribati islands are atoll chains in the Pacific Ocean.

★ **Sometimes, waves and wind** deposit small pieces of coral and sand on top of reefs. Over thousands of years, this debris piles up to form low-lying islands called cays.

★ **Coral cays** are known to support a variety of plant and animal life. Some cays eventually become small islands that people live on. However, other cays move across the reef and even disappear with time.

★ **Kiritimati**, or Christmas Island, is the largest coral atoll in the world. It is one of the Line Islands, a group of islands belonging to the Republic of Kiribati, which comprises 32 low-lying atolls and one raised island.

★ **Three of the four atolls** in the Caribbean Sea can be found off the coast of Belize, near Mexico. They are the Turneffe Atoll, Glover's Reef, and Lighthouse Reef.

★ **The Belize atolls** are unique. Unlike other atolls, these did not grow around volcanic islands. Instead, they developed on nonvolcanic ridges.

★ **The Coral Sea Islands**, off the east coast of Australia, are Australian territory. They are comprised of numerous small, uninhabited coral reefs and cays spread over an area of about 300,000 square miles.

▶ Coral reefs, which support a wide variety of marine life, are the largest ecosystems on our planet.

Icy waters

★ **The oceans** close to the North and South poles—the Arctic and the Antarctic—are partly frozen throughout the year.

★ **These oceans** are covered with dazzling white icebergs and huge sheets of floating ice, which make it difficult for ships to navigate these waters.

★ **The Antarctic Ocean** surrounds Antarctica, which is an island continent. The Arctic Ocean surrounds the North Pole.

▼ *The term "iceberg" has its origin in the German word* berg, *meaning "mountain."*

- **In winter**, the water close to the land is frozen. The ice melts in the summer and large chunks of ice, called icebergs, break off and float in the sea.

- **Massive slabs** of permanent ice, or ice shelves, break off and also float close to the shores in the Antarctic Ocean. The Ross Ice Shelf is the largest of these.

DID YOU KNOW?

Several polar fish have blood that is thickened by natural chemicals to keep it from freezing. Even if trapped in an area of solid ice, these fish can survive for a while by staying still and using little energy.

- **Unlike at the South Pole**, there is no landmass around the North Pole. Most parts of the Arctic Ocean are covered by ice sheets.

- **Apart from the Arctic** and Antarctic oceans, there are other seas that freeze during winter. The Okhotsk Sea and the Bering Sea, divided by the Kamchatka Peninsula in the northwestern Pacific region, remain frozen during the winter.

- **The water** in the polar regions might be freezing cold, but it is still home to a wide range of marine life. Whales, sharks, jellyfish, squid, seals, polar bears, and seabirds can be found living in and around these oceans.

- **The harsh climate** on the Antarctic continent, however, is not conducive to life. This region is largely uninhabited. Only scientists brave the cold to conduct research. However, Inuit peoples are known to live in the Arctic region.

The Arctic: a profile

🌟 **The Arctic region** is not a clearly defined area. All of the planet that falls inside the Arctic Circle is called "the Arctic." The Arctic Circle is the imaginary circle surrounding the North Pole. Unlike Antarctica, it is not a single landmass or continent.

🌟 **The North Pole** is in the middle of the Arctic Ocean. The ocean is surrounded by Russia, Greenland, Iceland, Canada, and Alaska.

🌟 **Contrary to popular belief**, the North Pole is not the coldest part of the Arctic region. Oymyakon in Siberia is actually the coldest, with a temperature of −90°F.

> **DID YOU KNOW?**
> In summer the North Pole has sunshine all day long, even at midnight, but in winter there is total darkness all day, even at midday.

🌟 **A large part of the land** surrounding the Arctic Ocean is extremely cold and treeless. This region is called the tundra. The word *tundra* is from the Finnish word *tunturia*, which means "barren land."

🌟 **The Arctic tundra** is so cold that the ground beneath the surface remains frozen throughout the year. This frozen ground is called permafrost. The topmost layer of the permafrost thaws every summer.

🌟 **The permafrost** does not allow plants to grow deep roots. Hence, the tundra is not suitable for trees. However, a large variety of mosses, lichens, shrubs, and small flowering plants can be found in this region.

✹ **The Arctic is home** to animals and birds such as the arctic fox, seals, orcas, beluga whales, Greenland sharks, polar bears, and caribou. However, not all creatures live in the region throughout the year. Many animals are only seen during the summer.

✹ **Inuit**, or Eskimos, are the original inhabitants of the Arctic region. The word *Eskimo* means "eater of raw meat" in Algonquian, a Native American language. Today these people prefer to be called Inuit, which means "the people" in the language Inuktitut.

✹ **Traditionally the Inuit** depended mostly on seals for survival, as the meat provided food, while the blubber was used as fuel and to make tents. In summer they traveled in kayaks, boats made from animal skin. In winter they used dogsleds.

✹ **Today, most Inuit live** in houses made of wood instead of igloos or tents. They wear modern clothing and travel in motorboats and snowmobiles. They also speak English, Russian, or Danish as well as their native tongue.

▼ *Temperatures in the Arctic are very low all year round. Nevertheless, people have lived here for over 10,000 years and still do today.*

Antarctica: a profile

* **Antarctica** is the fifth-largest continent. It lies at the southernmost point of the globe, and surrounds the South Pole.

* **This island continent** is surrounded by the icy Antarctic Ocean. The total area is about 5.4 million square miles in summer.

* **Antarctica** is roughly round in shape. Two seas, the Weddell Sea to the northwest and the Ross Sea to the southwest, cut into the continent.

* **Antarctica** was the last continent to be discovered. It is the most remote landmass, and by far the coldest and the windiest.

* **This continent** has the lowest temperatures on Earth. During winter, the temperature falls below −130°F.

* **Antarctica** receives no rainfall. It is often referred to as a cold desert. The snow hardly melts or evaporates. Instead, it accumulates in icy layers year after year.

* **The thick ice cover** makes Antarctica the highest of all continents, with an average height of about 7,500 feet. The ice covering this continent makes up 70 percent of the Earth's freshwater.

* **The continent** has been broadly divided into Greater Antarctica and West Antarctica. These areas are separated by the Transantarctic Mountains. A large portion of this mountain range is buried under ice.

* **At certain places**, taller parts of the Transantarctic Mountains manage to peek out of the ice. These tips of rocks, called *nunatak*, are often home to birds, such as snow petrels.

▼ Antarctica has been covered with ice for about five million years. It is home to large colonies of penguins.

DID YOU KNOW?

The Antarctic Treaty (1961) allows only peaceful activities such as scientific research on the continent and in its ocean.

Glaciers and icebergs

* **Glaciers are moving** masses of ice. They form on top of high mountains and in the polar regions, where temperatures are well below freezing point during winter and the summer is not warm enough to melt the snow.

* **Continuous snowfall** leads to the accumulation of snow. Each year, new layers of snow compress the previous layers, gradually forming ice.

* **Once the glacier** attains enough weight, it slowly starts sliding down a slope. Glaciers can be broadly divided into four types depending on where they were formed. These are icecap, alpine, piedmont, and continental glaciers.

DID YOU KNOW?

The part of an iceberg that is visible above water is only a small portion of its entire bulk. The enormous submerged part can be a great danger to ships. The saying "tip of the iceberg" has its origins in this phenomenon.

* **Alpine glaciers** originate from mountains and feed mountain rivers. Piedmont glaciers are formed when alpine glaciers join at the foot of a mountain.

* **A huge blanket** of ice and snow covers most of Greenland and Antarctica. These formations are known as continental glaciers, or ice sheets.

* **Icecap glaciers** are miniature versions of continental glaciers. They usually occupy elevated regions such as plateaus. Sometimes these icecaps break off at the edges and fall into the ocean.

★ **Icebergs are massive** chunks of ice that break off the ends of ice sheets, glaciers, and ice caps and then float into the sea.

★ **The largest icebergs** are formed from ice shelves. These shelves crack at the outer ends, and icebergs drift out to sea.

★ **The ice in some icebergs** contains tiny air bubbles that reflect light and give the iceberg a dazzling, white look. Ice that melts and freezes again can give the iceberg a blue tint.

★ **Icebergs** are of different shapes and sizes. They can be broadly classified as rounded, irregular, and tabular, or resembling a tabletop.

▼ *Snow and ice slide slowly from the polar ice caps as long glaciers, down to the sea.*

43

Polar life

⭐ **Extremely low temperatures** throughout the year make life difficult in the polar regions. Despite the cold, some plants and animals are able to survive in the Arctic and in Antarctica.

⭐ **Antarctica is covered** with a thick layer of ice throughout the year, making it impossible for large land animals to survive. However, microscopic organisms and small insects thrive here.

⭐ **Marine life** flourishes in the polar regions. Apart from numerous species of fish, animals such as jellyfish, starfish, squid, and sea anemones live in the Antarctic and Arctic oceans. Whales, sharks, dolphins, and seals are also found in these regions.

⭐ **Several species** of albatross, gulls, and petrels are found in Antarctica. However, this region is best known for its penguins. Arctic birds include puffins, gulls, snowy owls, petrels, auks, and guillemots.

⭐ **Polar bears and reindeer** are found only in the arctic region. Beluga whales and narwhals also thrive in the Arctic Ocean.

⭐ **The Arctic** is home to several other land animals. The arctic fox, brown bear, moose, wolf, ermine, musk ox, hare, and squirrel also live there.

⭐ **Lack of moisture** and low temperatures limit vegetation in the coldest parts of the polar regions. In Antarctica, land vegetation consists of algae, lichens, and moss.

⭐ **Coastal seaweeds** thrive in the southern waters of the Antarctic Ocean, along with some forms of marine algae.

⭐ **In the Arctic**, the tundra supports a wide variety of plant life, especially during spring. This includes shrubs, grass, moss, lichen, and certain species of flowering plants. Tall trees are unable to survive in these extreme conditions.

▶ Snowy owls make nests on the tundra. The female looks after the chicks while the male hunts for food.

Studying the oceans

The study of the chemical and physical properties of oceans and their ecosystems is called oceanography, oceanology, or marine science.

Oceanography comprises marine geology, physical oceanography, chemical oceanography, marine biology, and meteorological oceanography.

Marine geology deals with the study of tectonic plates in the earth's crust. These plates are responsible for natural phenomena such as volcanoes, earthquakes, mountains, and valleys.

▼ *A satellite photograph of a hurricane forming over the ocean. Meteorological oceanography deals with the influence of oceans on weather patterns across the world.*

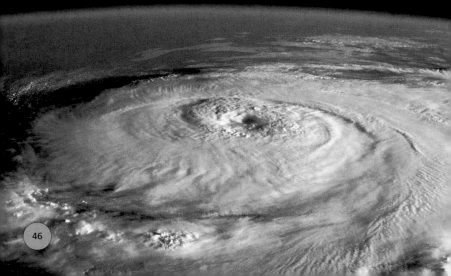

✦ **Apart from studying** the earth's crust and other related phenomena, marine geologists involved in offshore oil exploration and drilling also study how sediments and minerals are formed.

✦ **Physical oceanography** is the study of the physical processes that take place in the oceans. These include ocean currents, temperature, salt content in ocean water, and the causes of tides.

✦ **Chemical oceanography** is the study of chemicals in the oceans. The seas contain most of the elements found in the earth, including fossil fuels and minerals.

✦ **Oceanography** also includes allied sciences such as the study of caves, or speleology. This subject deals with the origin, physical structure, and development of caves. It also studies the flora and fauna of caves.

✦ **Hydrography** is another important branch of oceanography. It is the oldest science that deals with the sea and is defined as the study of water depth and quality, and of material found on the ocean floor, with specific reference to their impact on navigation.

✦ **Oceanography** gained importance with the age of discovery in 1400–1500. New lands were being discovered and oceans were mapped out during this time by explorers from great maritime nations such as Portugal and Spain.

✦ **Meteorological oceanography** deals with the interaction between the oceans and the atmosphere. It is the study of atmospheric reactions above the oceans and the influence of the oceans on global weather.

Oceans' treasure chest

★ **The oceans** are treasure troves of precious gems and metals. Apart from diamonds, salt, and other minerals, the oceans also contain vast reserves of oil.

★ **Pearls** are perhaps the first precious objects that come to mind when we think of the oceans.

▲ Nacre, the shiny substance that lines the insides of oyster shells, is also called "mother of pearl," since it is the main constituent of pearls.

⭐ **A pearl** is formed when a foreign object lodges itself inside the shell of an oyster, clam, or mussel. These creatures coat the object with a substance called nacre, which lines the inside of the shell.

⭐ **Nacre is deposited** in thin layers around the object, forming a pearl. Pearls are largely white or pale yellow in color. However, some can be black, gray, red, green, or blue.

⭐ **Most pearls** are smooth and round, but some turn out to be uneven in shape and might not be as valuable. These pearls are called baroque pearls and are increasingly being used to make jewelry.

⭐ **The seabed** is also a source of diamonds. These precious gems are found in the form of gravel on the seabed, especially in African and Indonesian waters.

⭐ **Offshore diamonds** are often of superior quality when compared to some onshore varieties. The ocean diamond mining industry is growing rapidly.

⭐ **The lure of gold** has also led people into the seas. Ocean water contains a large quantity of dissolved gold. However, the metal is difficult to extract since it is spread over a vast area.

⭐ **It is believed that** over 10 billion tons of gold can be found in dissolved form in the oceans. However, it is present in such low concentrations that it is not possible to recover it.

⭐ **Sand, gravel, and oyster shells** found on the ocean floor are widely used to make cement for construction purposes.

Mineral riches

✴ **The oceans** contain an abundant supply of useful minerals. However, their vastness and inaccessibility make it difficult to extract most of these resources.

✴ **Sodium chloride**, better known as common salt, is one of the major minerals that are obtained from the oceans. It accounts for 3 percent of the weight of the ocean water.

✴ **Salt deposits** are formed when ocean water evaporates. Some lakes and rivers also contain salt deposits and crusts.

✴ **Other major minerals** obtained from the oceans are magnesium and bromine. Magnesium and its compounds are used in the agricultural, construction, and chemical industries, while bromine is used in photography and disinfectants.

✴ **Sedimentary rocks** such as limestone, sandstone, and gypsum are also found in the oceans. These are formed by erosion due to the action of water on shells and the remains of marine creatures. They are used in building materials.

◄ *Sandstone that formed in the oceans can contain fossilized mollusk and brachiopod shells, trilobites, and ammonites.*

▶ *Limestone deposits often contain fossils of prehistoric marine creatures.*

★ **Certain phosphorous minerals,** such as phosphorite, are also found on the seabed. These have potential uses as agricultural fertilizers.

★ **Huge deposits** of manganese nodules have recently been discovered in the seabed, particularly in the Pacific Ocean. These nodules primarily consist of manganese and iron. Traces of copper, cobalt, and nickel can also be found in them.

★ **The oceans** are full of sulfur. Hydrothermal vents spout hot, sulfur-rich water that also has a high concentration of other metals and minerals. Sulfur is used in fertilizers, food preservatives, bleaching agents, and disinfectants.

★ **Mining the oceans** is expensive and not easy to do. There is an international dispute regarding the ownership of the oceans' mineral wealth.

★ **An international maritime law** clearly defines the rules of sharing mineral wealth of the oceans. However, the debate continues on whether a particular spot in an ocean belongs to the nearest countries or to the global community.

51

Fossil fuels

★ **Fossil fuels**, such as petroleum, coal, and natural gas, are extracted from the fossilized remains of animals and plants. These remains have been buried under layers of sediment, rock, and soil for millions of years.

★ **Crude oil**, which is refined to make petroleum, is formed from microscopic plants and organisms, such as bacteria, which lived in the ancient oceans.

★ **These microorganisms** died and mixed with the silt on the ocean floor to form organic mud. Layers of sediment settled on this organic ooze, transforming it into crude oil.

★ **Natural gas** is primarily formed by the decomposition or decaying of dead plankton that have accumulated on the ocean floor.

★ **Both crude oil** and natural gas fill porous rock nearby. This rock is called reservoir rock. Since reservoir rock is normally filled with water, the fuel, which is lighter than water, travels upward until it reaches a layer of nonporous rock.

★ **The nonporous rock** traps crude oil and natural gas to create a reservoir of fuel. Since natural gas is lighter than crude oil, it is found in a layer above the oil. Crude oil forms the middle layer, with water as the bottom layer.

★ **Coal is a solid fossil fuel** and is formed from decomposed plants that have hardened over the years. Coal is often found under the seabed, but offshore coal mining is not as widespread as that of oil and gas.

⭐ **Scientists** have found immense deposits of other hydrocarbon products, such as gas hydrates and oil shale, in the ocean floor.

⭐ **Gas hydrates** are crystals of methane, while oil shale is a rock containing a waxy compound called kerogen.

⭐ **Like crude oil**, oil shale is formed from dead microscopic organisms. Over the years, these organisms are transformed into kerogen. However, the temperature and pressure on the ocean floor are sometimes not high enough to convert kerogen into crude oil.

▼ Oil and natural gas formed from the remains of tiny prehistoric sea creatures that collected on the seabed. Layers of rock built up on top and squashed them. Over time, they became underground stores of oil, with pockets of gas above.

Oil platform drilling for oil and gas

Hard rock layer

Gas

Oil

Oil and gas move upward through soft rock layers until reaching a hard rock layer.

The layer of dead sea creatures is crushed by rock that forms above, and turns into oil and gas.

Tiny sea creatures die and sink to the seabed.

Drilling for oil

⭐ **With dwindling land resources**, the search for oil in the oceans is increasing. Natural resources found in the seabed are extracted and refined to produce fuel.

⭐ **Oil companies** usually build offshore drilling rigs to extract resources from the seabed. Rigs are platforms set up in the sea at a distance from the shore.

⭐ **Oil rigs** are tough structures made of steel or concrete that can withstand huge waves and storms. Alaskan oil rigs also have to withstand icy waters and ice floes.

▼ The oil platform's welded-steel legs rest on the seabed. They support the platform around 50 feet above the surface of the water.

★ **These rigs** are equipped with massive, tubular drills that dig several hundred feet into the ocean floor. The samples brought up by these pipes are then tested for signs of crude oil.

★ **Once the existence** of crude oil is confirmed, it is extracted and sent to refineries, where it is refined into petroleum and petroleum products, such as gasoline.

DID YOU KNOW?

Permanent oil rigs sometimes support an ecosystem. Their underwater structures form artificial reefs, with plenty of marine creatures living on them. Some offshore platforms are popular spots for rig diving.

★ **Some oil rigs** are huge platforms that drop an anchor and float on the water. These platforms have air-filled supports, and are called semisubmersible rigs.

★ **Permanent oil rigs** are built in places where production is high and multiple oil wells can be drilled. Some of these rigs, measuring over 425 feet in diameter and almost 800 feet high, are held in place by concrete or steel legs.

★ **Sometimes pressure** builds up in the underground wells, causing blowouts. When a blowout occurs, the drilling hole explodes, spilling oil into the surrounding waters.

★ **Mud, pipes, and rocks** are also thrown into the air during a blowout. Oil spills are harmful to the environment. Apart from polluting the water, they also destroy marine life.

★ **Blowout preventers** control pressure in underwater wells while drilling.

Pollution

* **People have exploited oceans** for their vast resources since ancient times. Excessive human activity in coastal areas has increased pollution and caused irreparable damage to ocean life.

* **Discharge** of industrial waste and human sewage into the sea is the most common form of pollution. This affects marine creatures and makes the sea unfit for swimming.

* **The pollution** that enters oceans can be categorized as coming from "point sources" and "nonpoint sources." Sewer pipes and industrial waste pipes are point sources, as the discharge is from a single, identifiable point.

* **Nonpoint sources** of pollution are more difficult to tackle. These include water or sewage from farms containing fertilizers with a high chemical content.

* **Some chemicals** found in pesticides are biodegradable, and their effects are minimal and short-lived. Others remain dangerous for a long time.

* **Petroleum** and oil products are major pollutants that enter the water through spills from ships and leakages from pipelines, tankers, and storage tanks.

* **Water discharged from power plants** causes thermal pollution. It is usually hot and so it alters the temperature of the seawater, affecting marine life adversely.

* **Populations** of some animals, such as dolphins, beluga whales, manatees, and polar bears, have been diminished by industrial pollution and farm wastes.

⭐ **Many beaches** have become tourist attractions. Plastic litter left on tourist beaches is a great hazard to marine life, proving fatal to some creatures.

⭐ **Metals such as copper**, mercury, selenium, and lead enter the oceans from industrial waste and automobile emissions. These can cause long-term health problems in both animals and humans.

▼ *This ship is discharging waste straight into the ocean that may prove fatal to many forms of marine life.*

57

Oil spills

✴ **The worst form of ocean pollution** is oil spills. The effects are long lasting and extremely damaging.

✴ **Oil spills** are usually caused when large ocean tankers have accidents while transporting their liquid cargo.

▲ Although oil tanker accidents are considered to be detrimental to marine life, they account for barely 5 percent of the total oil that flows into the oceans. The main oil pollutants are oil refineries and ships that wash their tanks at sea.

★ **Oil does not mix** with water. During an oil spill, the oil spreads very fast, forming a thin, filmlike layer on the water's surface. This layer is known as an "oil slick."

★ **Oil also gets** into the oceans from pipelines and leaky underground storage tanks. Heavier components of crude oil, such as polynuclear aromatic hydrocarbons, cause the most damage.

★ **Oil slicks** are very harmful to marine life, as well as to birds and mammals living near the oceans. Oil damages the water-repellent properties in the fur of mammals like sea otters and the wings of birds.

★ **Coral reefs**, mangroves, and estuaries are sensitive to oil spills.

★ **The effects of oil spills** are not always immediate and the harm caused may last long afterward. Oil spills often cause diseases of the liver, and reproductive and growth problems in marine creatures.

★ **The oil tanker** *Exxon Valdez* ran aground in 1989, dumping more than 10 million gallons of oil into Prince William Sound, off the coast of Alaska. The damage caused was the worst in history.

★ **The environmental damage** caused by the *Exxon Valdez* prompted the United States Congress to pass safety laws for oil tankers and barges. Oil companies were also made responsible for spill cleanup.

★ **Another huge oil spill** occurred in 1978 when the American supertanker *Amoco Cadiz* ran aground off the coast of Brittany, France. The spill resulted in one of the largest-ever losses of marine life.

Greenhouse effect

★ **Rapid industrial development** and population growth are taking their toll on the oceans. Some of the factors affecting marine life and the environment include chemical pollution, global warming, oil spills, and overfishing.

★ **Global warming** can have an alarming effect on oceans and, thus, on life on earth. The increase in temperature of the planet's atmosphere and the oceans is called global warming. Some scientists believe that it is the direct result of the greenhouse effect.

★ **The sun's heat** is absorbed by the earth's atmosphere and radiated back into space. Certain gases in the earth's atmosphere trap a part of this reflected heat, thus keeping the earth warm. This process is termed "natural greenhouse effect."

★ **The greenhouse effect** is similar to what happens in a greenhouse filled with plants. The surrounding glass allows sunlight in but blocks the heat from going out, thus keeping the temperature warm even when it becomes cold outside.

★ **Greenhouse gases** in the atmosphere include water vapor, carbon dioxide, methane, nitrous oxide, ozone, and chlorofluorocarbons (CFCs). The amount of greenhouse gases in the atmosphere determines the amount of trapped heat.

★ **Water vapor** is the most important greenhouse gas. It is responsible for over 60 percent of the greenhouse effect. Carbon dioxide is the other significant contributor. Chlorofluorocarbons can trap more heat than any other greenhouse gas, but very little of these exist in the atmosphere.

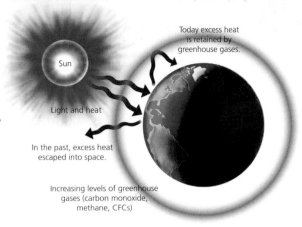

Today excess heat is retained by greenhouse gases.

Sun

Light and heat

▶ While a large part of the sun's heat is reflected back by the earth's surface, some of it is trapped by the greenhouse gases in the atmosphere.

In the past, excess heat escaped into space.

Increasing levels of greenhouse gases (carbon monoxide, methane, CFCs)

⭐ **Greenhouse gases** in normal quantities are essential, since they provide insulation to the earth and help sustain life. Industrialization has increased the level of greenhouse gases in the atmosphere, thus trapping more heat than is required. This is called the "enhanced greenhouse effect."

⭐ **Human activity** has contributed greatly to the increase in the amount of greenhouse gases. The major factor is carbon dioxide emission from fossil fuel combustion.

⭐ **Deforestation** contributes heavily to the increased levels of carbon dioxide in the atmosphere. Trees that have been cut down release carbon dioxide as they decay.

⭐ **Global warming** can cause significant changes in the climatic conditions across the world, thus affecting life on our planet. An increase in temperatures would lead to faster rates of evaporation, the melting of glaciers and polar ice caps, and a rise in sea levels. It would also have an adverse effect on agriculture.

Oceans in danger

🌟 **Oceans**, which occupy about 70 percent of the earth's surface, absorb much of the solar heat and are therefore the most affected by global warming.

🌟 **Scientists believe** that the enhanced greenhouse effect could cause more water to be formed, due to the melting of glaciers and ice caps, than is possible naturally.

🌟 **Global warming** caused by greenhouse gases has increased the earth's surface temperature by about 1.3 degrees Fahrenheit over the last century.

🌟 **Higher surface temperatures** can melt mountain glaciers and parts of polar ice caps, causing the sea level to go up by 3 feet within a century or two.

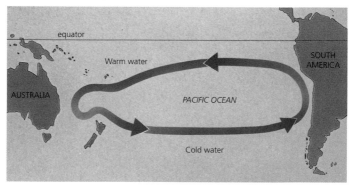

equator

Warm water

SOUTH AMERICA

AUSTRALIA

PACIFIC OCEAN

Cold water

▲ *High atmospheric pressure develops over the Pacific Ocean, which causes trade winds to blow from east to west, carrying warm surface waters toward the west. This is called the El Niño effect and usually occurs during December.*

★ **This could** have a dangerous effect on the coastlines and the people living in these regions. Many marine species could become extinct if global warming is not checked.

★ **El Niño**, a sudden surge of warm waters off the west coast of South America, is a significant climatic phenomenon some scientists attribute to global warming.

★ **Oceans play an important role** in controlling the weather. Hence, an increase in their surface temperature will also affect weather patterns. Prolonged drought or increased flooding can wreak havoc on landmasses.

★ **Global warming** is also responsible for the melting of sea ice and ice caps in the polar regions. According to recent studies, glaciers along the coast of Greenland are becoming thinner by about 3 feet every year. The melting of glaciers and sea ice can also increase sea levels, thus reducing coastlines and beaches.

★ **Oceans** are considered to be biological pumps for carbon dioxide. They are full of microscopic phytoplanktons, which remove almost half of the natural carbon dioxide formed. Any change in their habitat may lead to further damage, thus directly increasing the amount of carbon dioxide in the atmosphere.

★ **Sensing the dangers**, many nations have finally swung into action to save the environment. The Kyoto Protocol, adopted in December 1997, requires the 127 countries that have signed it to take effective measures in order to reduce the amount of greenhouse gases in the atmosphere by 2012.

Sinking lands

★ **The sea level** has already increased rapidly in the last 100 years due to global warming, with many coastal and low-lying areas threatened by flooding.

★ **The major reason** for the rise in the level of the sea is the melting of the Arctic and Antarctic ice packs. The thickness of these packs has reduced in the last century, adding to the volume of water in the oceans.

★ **Scientists predict** that the level of the oceans will rise more dramatically over the next 100 years, with temperatures expected to rise by almost eight degrees Fahrenheit.

★ **Many major cities** of the world, such as New York, Los Angeles, Rio de Janeiro, London, and Singapore, lie in coastal areas or near river mouths.

★ **The constant melting** of mountain glaciers and ice packs could threaten these cities with flooding.

★ **Scientists** believe that even a 20-inch rise in the sea level will affect millions of people in Bangladesh, India, and Vietnam.

★ **The population** of small island-states, such as the Seychelles, the Maldives, and Tuvalu, will be seriously affected by a rise in the sea level, since these countries are only a few feet above it.

★ **Tuvalu** is a group of nine coral atolls that lie in the Pacific Ocean, just 16 feet above sea level. It is predicted that if the present situation continues, then these atolls will be completely submerged within 50 years.

★ **Many ecologically sensitive zones**, such as the Everglades in Florida, will become submerged.

★ **The rising temperatures** are also destroying shallow-water marine life. Global warming is said to be responsible for the destruction of coral reefs in Belize. Even the Great Barrier Reef off the coast of Australia is now in grave danger.

▼ *The rising sea levels may cause coral reefs, such as the Great Barrier Reef, to become submerged.*

Crowding the coasts

⭐ **Coastal regions** are important for many reasons. The land along coasts is usually very fertile and therefore good for farming. The beaches also attract many tourists to coastal areas.

⭐ **Since ancient times**, humans have made coastal areas their homes. Almost half of the world's population lives close to the coasts.

▲ *Littering of coastal areas is one of the most common problems today. Tourists who visit coastal regions do not give much thought to the consequences of leaving behind debris such as plastic items.*

- **Most coastal regions** have, as a result, become overcrowded. This has led to pollution, damaged ecosystems, and eroded coastlines.

- **People have built houses** and factories that discharge sewage and industrial waste into the seas. These damage the shores and pollute the oceans.

- **Industrial waste** contaminates popular beaches and poisons shellfish beds. It also destroys natural habitats and has adverse affects on human health.

- **The development of ports** and roads, coastal construction, and mining of sand for construction material are destroying coastal habitats like coral reefs.

- **The shore** has also been damaged by attempts to control the movement of sediment such as sand and shingle. This prevents erosion in some places but leads to deposition of sediments in other areas.

- **Jetties and breakwaters** are built to protect harbor entrances and maintain a constant depth of water. These structures block the natural drift of sediment.

- **Artificial beaches** are built to reclaim land from the sea, damaging the coast beyond repair. Offshore dredging of sand to build beaches adds to the problem.

- **To attract tourists**, hotels and apartments are often built close to the water. This makes such areas vulnerable to pollution and disturbs the natural marine habitats and marine life.

Bleaching the reefs

⭐ **The impact** of global warming on the oceans is most notable in the bleaching of coral reefs.

⭐ **Reefs are very delicate** and sensitive structures formed by coral polyps. Although polyps feed on passing plankton, their main source of food is the unicellular algae called zooxanthellae, which live within their tissues.

⭐ **The algae feed** on the nitrogen waste produced by the corals. Like all plants, zooxanthellae also produce food using sunlight. It is this that forms the main food of corals.

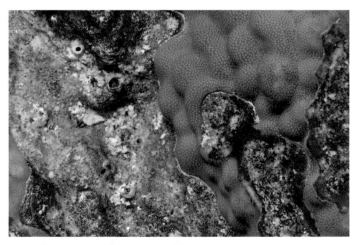

▲ Both hard corals and non-reef-building corals, or soft corals, are susceptible to bleaching. Soft corals are able to withstand short-term bleaching much better than hard corals.

- **Zooxanthellae** also provide the reefs with their magnificent coloring, which attracts many other marine creatures, thus forming an ecosystem.

- **Reefs lose color** and die when these zooxanthellae are damaged. This is known as bleaching.

DID YOU KNOW?

Bleaching is dangerous because it affects not only the coral reefs but also a large number of marine creatures that depend on them for food.

- **Global warming** is the main cause of bleaching. A rise in the temperature of the oceans interferes with the photosynthetic process, eventually poisoning the zooxanthellae. Corals, in turn, are forced to expel the dead zooxanthellae, along with some of their own tissue.

- **Once the algae are expelled**, the corals lose their color and main source of food. Unless the algae are able to grow again, the corals will gradually starve to death.

- **Widespread bleaching** took place at reefs around Okinawa, Easter Island, and in the Caribbean Sea in 1979 and 1980. The Great Barrier Reef has also undergone bleaching in the last 20 years.

- **Some of the coral reefs** that have been permanently damaged are in the warm waters of the Indian Ocean, including those off the coasts of the Maldives, Sri Lanka, Kenya, and Tanzania.

- **Bleached coral reefs** take years to recuperate. Sometimes they get bleached again before they can fully recover from the first attack.

Endangered species

★ **Endangered species** are animals and plants that are facing extinction. These species will die out if nothing is done to keep them alive.

★ **The main reasons** for a species becoming endangered are the destruction of their habitat by people, pollution, and commercial exploitation by way of hunting and trade in animal parts.

★ **Around 34,000 plant species** and 5,200 animal species are close to extinction.

★ **The current rate** of extinction is thought to be around 20,000 species every year. Studies suggest that this is the first age of mass extinction since the dinosaurs disappeared nearly 65 million years ago.

★ **When their habitats are destroyed**, many animals are not able to adapt quickly enough to the changed surroundings, which eventually leads to their extinction.

★ **For marine life**, pollution and hunting are the major causes of extinction and endangerment. Excessive hunting has greatly reduced the numbers of sea turtles. Sea turtle eggs are a favorite food of both humans and animals.

★ **Between the 1800s and the early 1900s**, whales were killed in large numbers for their meat and blubber. This led to the endangerment of many whale species.

★ **Higher water temperatures**, along with pollution, have endangered several fish species. Oil spills kill many birds, fish, and marine mammals.

⭐ **Changes in biodiversity** can also lead to extinction. Biodiversity is where particular species thrive and depend on each other.

⭐ **The kelp forest** in the North Pacific used to be one of the richest biodiversity zones. When humans killed sea otters in large numbers, the population of sea urchins, the main food of sea otters, increased. The sea urchins then ate much more of the kelp, leading to the collapse of the entire ecosystem.

▼ *Polar bears rely on ice floes to hunt seals—their main food source. Melting ice means it is harder to hunt seals, and so the bears starve.*

71

Whaling and fishing

* **Whaling is the commercial hunting** of whales for oil, meat, whalebone, and other products. Whaling activity is believed to have begun in western Europe around the 900s.

* **In the 1100s**, whales were hunted off the coasts of Spain and Germany until their numbers were drastically depleted. Whaling in North America began with its colonization and was at an all-time high by the 1700s.

* **In the early 19th century**, whales were usually killed by harpoons and other weapons. Whaling became easier with the arrival of large boats, called factory ships, which were equipped with machinery to process slaughtered whales.

▼ In this early 19th-century scene, a harpooner takes aim at a right whale from his rowboat. The main hunting boat approaches in the distance.

- **Sperm whales** were killed mainly for the type of oil that they produced, known as spermaceti. This was used as a lubricant and in medicines.

- **The International Whaling Commission** was established in 1946, when whale populations began falling alarmingly. It regulated the hunting of whales, eventually leading to an increase in their numbers.

DID YOU KNOW?
Sport fishing, also called angling, is one of the most popular recreational activities in the world. Anglers use fishing rods and lines to catch game fish like marlin and swordfish.

- **Fishing is one** of the biggest commercial activities carried out in the oceans. Fish are caught in large numbers to meet ever-growing demands. They are valuable protein sources.

- **Mackerel, herring, and tuna** are among the most caught and eaten fish around the world. Sharks are considered a delicacy in some parts of the world. Shellfish such as shrimp and lobster are also popular.

- **Overfishing** has led to the endangerment of many fish species, such as cod, mackerel, and tuna.

- **The increasing world demand** for fish has led to the development of fish farms, where fish are grown and harvested for food.

- **Fish farming** provides about 20 percent of all fish eaten— salmon, shrimp, and carp are the most harvested. China leads the world in fish farming.

Saving ocean life

🌟 **Many marine species** have already become extinct, while several more are endangered.

🌟 **Destruction of habitats**, pollution, and overfishing are the main reasons for this. Efforts are being undertaken around the world to save marine creatures.

🌟 **Some ocean regions** are being specially protected. Fishing and other activities that disturb marine life in these areas are prohibited.

🌟 **These regions** have been established as safe havens for endangered species and for the protection of commercial fish stocks.

🌟 **Only 1 percent** of the world's oceans, however, are protected. Many organizations, like the World Wildlife Fund, are trying to increase the coverage of protected areas.

🌟 **Some habitats** are protected by the prohibition of destructive fishing gear. This ensures the development of the ecosystem, thus allowing fish species to grow to their normal size and produce more offspring.

🌟 **The Great Barrier Reef** is one of the largest protected marine ecosystems. Commercial fishing and bleaching have destroyed vast stretches of these reefs.

🌟 **Drilling for minerals**, oil, or gas continues to pose a major threat to sensitive habitats. Efforts are being made to persuade companies to use methods that do not harm sea life.

⭐ **Ecotourism**, which brings people who are concerned about the environment to areas of natural beauty, is helping to fund conservation projects.

⭐ **The population** of endangered marine species is being increased by many projects. Turtles, sharks, and dolphins, for example, are being bred artificially under controlled conditions and then let out into the open seas.

▲ *These dead fish are the result of chemical pollution. Thousands of marine creatures are washed ashore every year.*

Cleaning the oceans

⭐ **People are directly responsible** for the dangers facing the oceans today. Our increasing demands have resulted in endangered marine animals, damaged ecosystems, melting ice caps, and polluted seas.

⭐ **The value** of the oceans' resources is now being recognized. Efforts are being made across the world to control the deterioration. Some nations are spending large amounts of money to protect the oceans.

⭐ **The biggest problem** facing the oceans is global warming. Reducing the emission of greenhouse gases could stop global warming. Cleaner energy sources will control the release of carbon dioxide into the atmosphere.

◄ Sorbents, or large sponges, are used in the final stages of an oil spill cleanup. These materials can absorb oil effectively, especially from beaches.

🌟 **The Kyoto Protocol**, a treaty aimed at reducing the release of greenhouse gases, has been agreed on by many nations. However, some of the largest polluting nations, such as the United States, have yet to sign it.

🌟 **The harm caused** by synthetic chemicals and fertilizers that run into the oceans is being reversed by the use of eco-friendly chemicals. These chemicals are biodegradable, which means that they decompose in a harmless way.

🌟 **New devices** are being developed to absorb oil spills, which are one of the biggest threats to marine life. Heavier oil products often settle to the bottom of oceans, killing fragile, bottom-dwelling marine creatures.

🌟 **Oil spills** are cleaned using booms, skimmers, and chemical dispersants. On shore, low- or high-pressure water hoses and vacuum trucks are also used.

🌟 **Floating barriers**, called "booms," are placed around oil spills or their sources to prevent the oil from spreading further. Skimmers are boats with plastic ropes that skim over the surface, absorbing the oil after the booms have been set up.

🌟 **Chemical dispersants** break down oil into its chemical constituents, thus making it less harmful to the marine environment.

🌟 **To save coastlines**, many nations are imposing strict building regulations. Construction activity and tourism have damaged many coastal ecosystems.

Ocean life

Early marine life

* **It is believed** that life on earth originated in the oceans around 3.8 billion years ago.

* **According to some scientists**, repeated lightning strikes triggered a reaction among certain compounds and gases in the earth's atmosphere. This reaction might have led to the formation of proteins and enzymes, which are the building blocks of life.

* **The proteins and enzymes** rained down on the oceans and developed into primitive single-celled organisms.

* **Around 620 million years ago**, complex and soft-bodied life-forms appeared for the first time.

* **Some of the earliest creatures** looked like modern jellyfish. They were very small and had a variety of shapes.

* **These early animals** soon evolved into more complex life-forms that are recognized today. Some of these early creatures included sponges, jellyfish, corals, flatworms, and mollusks.

* **The earliest fish** appeared around 480 million years ago. These were the jawless fish. The modern hagfish and lamprey are the only surviving members of this group.

* **Around 450 million years ago**, sharks and bony fish began to evolve. The first bony fish were small and had armored plates for defense.

⭐ **The early bony fish** were either ray-finned or lobe-finned. The coelacanth and the modern lungfish are the only lobe-finned fish that survive today.

⭐ **Most scientists** believe that lobe-finned fish used their fins to come out of the water for very short periods. This led to the evolution of amphibians, which themselves eventually evolved into other land creatures.

▼ *Coelacanths are referred to as "living fossils" because they have changed very little over millions of years.*

Modern marine life

* **The first modern fish** appeared around 250 million years ago. The ancient ray-finned fish gave rise to the neopterygians, which are considered to be ancestors of the modern fish.

* **Oceans today** are no different from the primitive oceans in terms of the number of creatures that live there. They are home to dozens of species of mammals and reptiles, innumerable small creatures, and more than 20,000 species of fish.

* **Oceans are divided** into two regions—the benthic zone, or the ocean floor, and the pelagic zone, which is the vast expanse of water. The pelagic zone is further divided into three zones. The topmost zone, called the epipelagic zone, supports around 90 percent of marine life.

* **The epipelagic zone** is the only ocean zone that gets sunlight. Apart from plants, many species of fish, reptiles, and mammals dwell in the epipelagic zone.

* **Very little sunlight** reaches the twilight zone, which is below the epipelagic zone, making it impossible for plants to survive. However, animals such as octopus, squid, hatchet fish, and viperfish are found in this zone.

* **Some animals** that live in the twilight zone are bioluminescent. Special organs, called photophores, in the bodies of these animals give off a greenish light.

* **The midnight zone** is the lowest zone and is completely dark and extremely cold. Very few creatures live in this zone and most of them do not have eyes.

⭐ **Oceans are among** the most productive ecosystems. Tiny plants and animals that float on the surface, called plankton, form the base of the oceanic food chain. Many land creatures, such as seabirds and polar bears, depend on oceans for survival.

▼ Oceans are home to nearly 300,000 different living species, ranging from huge whales to tiny fish.

1 Dusky dolphin	**8** Ocean sunfish	**14** Banded sea snake
2 Kittiwake	**9** Ridley's turtle	**15** Yellowfin tuna
3 Northern right whale	**10** Cuttlefish	**16** Common squid
4 Man 'o' war jellyfish	**11** Tiger shark	**17** Mako shark
5 Great skuas	**12** Yellow-bellied	**18** Nautilus
6 Pacific white-sided dolphin	sea snake	**19** Commerson's dolphin
7 Broad-billed prion	**13** Tarpon	**20** Sei whale

Marine biology

★ **Marine biology** is the study of life in the oceans and other related environments, such as estuaries and lagoons.

★ **Biological oceanography** and marine biology are often confused with each other. Both study marine creatures. However, biological oceanography studies the effects of a changing ocean environment on marine life.

★ **Marine biology** includes several other subfields, such as aquaculture, environmental marine biology, deep-sea ecology, ichthyology, marine mammology, and marine ethology.

★ **Environmental marine biology** is the study of the health of oceans and the effect of coastal development on the marine environment. It also looks at the impact of pollutants, such as oil spills and other chemical hazards, on the surrounding marine life.

★ **Deep-sea ecology** takes a closer look at how water creatures in the deep adapt to the dark and cold environment.

★ **Ichthyology** is the study of fish—both marine and freshwater.

★ **Marine mammology** is a relatively new subject that deals exclusively with the study of marine mammals such as whales, dolphins, and seals.

DID YOU KNOW?

Greek philosopher Aristotle was the first person to record detailed descriptions of marine life. He identified various species, including mollusks, fish, and crustaceans. He also classified whales and dolphins as mammals.

▲ *Ichthyologists deal with various aspects of fish, such as their classification, behavior, evolution, and habitats.*

Marine ethology helps us understand the behavior of marine animals in their natural environment. It also focuses on ways to save endangered species whose habitats are threatened by human activity or changes in the environment.

Marine biologists use various advanced methods to collect data for their research. Several new tools, such as plankton nets, remotely operated vehicles, and fiber optics have made studying the oceans much easier.

Artificial underwater habitats are built about 65 feet below the water's surface to accommodate scientists who work underwater for long periods.

Sponges

⭐ **Sponges might look like plants** but they are, in fact, animals. While most sponges are found in the sea, some species live in freshwater.

⭐ **These animals do not have eyes**, ears, a head, arms, legs, or any organs. Their bodies have thousands of pores that help them filter food from the water.

⭐ **Various shapes, sizes, and colors** of sponges have evolved. They can be extremely small or as wide as 13 feet in diameter.

◄ *Growing on top of this vase sponge is an echinoderm called a sea lily or crinoid, which is a stalked, upside-down version of its close cousin the starfish.*

* **Sponges cannot move about.** They attach themselves to solid objects, such as shells or stones, in places where food is abundant.

* **They do not have mouths.** Water containing tiny bits of food is drawn in through pores called ostia. After the nutrients are extracted, the water is released through a bigger opening, or osculum, at the top.

▲ The canals and chambers of sponges are home to a variety of small creatures, such as sea slugs, crabs, and shrimps.

* **A network of canals and chambers** inside the sponges help them to pump enormous quantities of water.

* **Certain deep-sea sponges** have spiky, hook-shaped filaments. When tiny crustaceans, like shrimps, get caught in these filaments, new ones grow around the prey to digest it. It takes a whole day for new filaments to envelop the prey.

* **There are around 10,000 species of sponges.** The barrel sponge is the biggest of all. It is so big that a full-grown human could climb into it. The tube sponge is a common colorful variety and is found mostly on reefs.

* **The red tree sponge** is extremely attractive. It is often confused with corals because of its bright, flowerlike structure.

* **The skeletons** of certain sponges are made up of a soft, silky substance called spongin. When these sponges die, their flexible skeletons are cleaned and bleached for use as bath sponges.

Coral reefs

⭐ **Colonies of coral polyps** form coral reefs. A coral polyp is a tiny animal that uses minerals in the sea to produce a protective outer skeleton. These skeletons form hard, branching structures called coral reefs.

⭐ **Coral polyps** eat algae. They also use their tentacles to capture tiny creatures called zooplankton.

⭐ **Corals** are ancient animals that have been around for 250 million years.

⭐ **Numerous sea animals** make their homes in coral reefs. Starfish, reef sharks, sponges, jellyfish, crabs, lobsters, anemones, eels, and a huge variety of fish add to the color of coral reefs.

⭐ **Coral reefs are found** in warm and shallow waters, usually within 30 degrees north and south of the equator.

⭐ **There are three kinds** of coral reefs. These are fringing and barrier reefs, and coral atolls.

⭐ **Fringing reefs** extend from the land into the sea. Barrier reefs are found farther from the shore, separated from the mainland by a lagoon. Atolls are ring-shaped formations of coral islands around a lagoon.

DID YOU KNOW?

The stinging hydroid coral found in the Indian and Pacific oceans uses special chemicals to paralyze plankton, which forms a major part of its diet.

2

★ **The Great Barrier Reef** in the Coral Sea off the northeastern coast of Australia is the biggest of all coral reefs. It is over 1,200 miles long.

★ **Coral reefs** are also found in the Indian Ocean and the Red Sea. Some of them also stretch along the Atlantic Ocean from Florida to the Caribbean Sea and Brazil.

★ **Coral reefs**, especially the Great Barrier Reef, are major tourist attractions because of their fascinating structures, vibrant colors, and rich marine life.

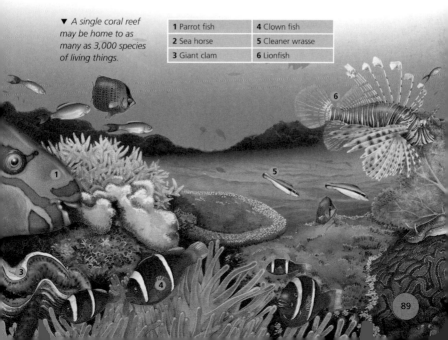

▼ A single coral reef may be home to as many as 3,000 species of living things.

1 Parrot fish	4 Clown fish
2 Sea horse	5 Cleaner wrasse
3 Giant clam	6 Lionfish

Symbiosis

⭐ **A unique bonding**, known as symbiosis, exists among certain animals. This refers to the dependence of two species on each other for food, protection, cleaning, or transportation.

⭐ **Symbiosis occurs** in many habitats, although it is more prevalent in the oceans.

⭐ **Based on** the kind of relationship that the animals share, symbiosis is divided into three main categories. These are mutualism, commensalism, and parasitism.

⭐ **A relationship** in which both creatures benefit is known as mutualism. This kind of bonding helps them survive in extreme conditions.

⭐ **A well-known example** of mutualism is the relationship between the sea anemone and the clown fish. The sea anemone's poisonous tentacles protect the clown fish, which lives among them. The fish returns the favor by keeping the tentacles clean.

⭐ **Cleaner fish**, like gobies, wrasse, and shrimps, also represent mutualism. These fish are found at the "cleaning stations" in coral reefs, where they clean bigger fish by removing parasites, dead skin, and tissue.

⭐ **In commensalism**, one species benefits while the other is unaffected. For example, remoras attach themselves to sharks and get a free ride. They also feed on the scraps of their hosts.

⭐ **In parasitism**, one species benefits at the expense of the other. The one that benefits is called a parasite.

⭐ **Parasites can be found** inside or on the body of the host. External parasites are called ectoparasites, while those found inside the body are called endoparasites.

⭐ **Lice and barnacles** that attach themselves to the body of whales and turtles are examples of ectoparasites.

▼ *Cleaner wrasse gather around the mouth and gill slits of this whitetip reef shark.*

91

Sea anemones

Sea anemones are colorful creatures that are sometimes confused with coral polyps.

Unlike corals, sea anemones do not have a skeleton to protect them. They attach themselves to solid surfaces, such as the seabed, corals, or rocks.

These creatures are most commonly found in tropical waters. They do not live in colonies like corals.

▼ The tentacles of sea anemones make them look like bright underwater flowers.

- **Sea anemones** are mostly stationary creatures. Those which move about do so very slowly by sliding. Swimming anemones look like rolling balls of tentacles.

- **Most sea anemones** are very small, but some varieties may grow to more than 3 feet in diameter. They have a cylindrical body and an opening at the top that serves as the mouth.

DID YOU KNOW?

The clown fish is quite safe living among sea anemones, despite their poisonous tentacles. The fish has a thick coating of slime that protects it against the anemone's sting, which does, however, deter the clown fish's predators.

- **The mouth** of a sea anemone is surrounded by tentacles. These tentacles are used to grab food and for defense.

- **The tentacles** have stinging cells that paralyze the sea anemone's prey. They also carry the prey into the sea anemone's mouth. Sticky mucus on the tentacles means they can grab even the smallest of fish.

- **Sea anemones** have a symbiotic relationship with the hermit crab. Since the sea anemone cannot travel very easily, it rides piggyback on the crab. The anemone is transported, while the crab gets protection from its enemies.

- **To prevent** their bodies from drying out, sea anemones that live in shallow waters secrete mucus or dig into the wet sand.

- **Anemones** can live for 70–100 years. Because of their vibrant colors, they are much sought-after for display in aquariums.

Jellyfish

- **Jellyfish** are found in oceans across the world. They are shaped like a bell and have poisonous tentacles.

- **The body** of a jellyfish is soft and does not have a fixed form. Its skin is almost transparent, as nearly 98 percent of its body is made up of water.

- **Jellyfish depend** on sea currents to drift about. They can swim a little, but this is limited to upward and downward movements.

- **Some species of jellyfish** can be very small, while others, such as the lion's mane, can grow to 8 feet in diameter.

- **Jellyfish** have a central cavity in their hood that acts as stomach and intestine. They eat plankton, other jellyfish, and small fish. Jellyfish use stinging tentacles to grab their prey.

- **When disturbed**, jellyfish emit a pale white light. Their senses are poorly developed, but special light sensors help them find their way around.

- **These sea animals** do not have gills or lungs. Oxygen is absorbed and carbon dioxide is released through their membranelike skin.

- **Most marine creatures** do not attack jellyfish. However, they are eaten by arrow crabs, sea turtles, and sunfish. Some people eat them, and the mushroom jellyfish is a delicacy in Japan and China.

- **Jellyfish have a complex** life cycle. They start their life as swimming larvae. The larvae attach themselves to the seabed and form a colony of polyps. Later, these polyps grow into bell-shaped structures and start drifting.

⭐ **The tentacles** of jellyfish are lined with hundreds of tiny stinging cells called nematocysts. These cells contain poison. The stings of some jellyfish, like the box jellyfish, can kill a full-grown human.

▼ Jellyfish move by squeezing water from beneath their bodies. When a jellyfish stops squeezing, it slowly sinks.

Starfish

★ **Also known as sea stars**, starfish are not fish. They are spiny creatures without bones. Most starfish have five arms, but some species have seven or 14 arms.

★ **Starfish** have developed a unique way of moving. They have hundreds of tiny, tubelike feet underneath their arms, which help them to crawl.

★ **The diet of starfish** includes oysters, fish, clams, and even waste deposits on the seabed.

★ **The mouth** of the starfish is underneath its body. If the prey is big, a starfish pushes its stomach out of its mouth to grab and digest the food.

▼ Starfish are found in most of the oceans across the world. They live on the seabed and can be many different sizes and colors.

▶ *Starfish are usually active at night. Some species eat corals and shellfish.*

Starfish do not have eyes. Instead, they have a small eyespot at the tip of each arm. The eyespots are linked to a network of nerves. Starfish also have good senses of touch and smell.

Some starfish can regenerate lost arms. A new starfish may be regenerated from a single arm attached to part of the central disk.

To reproduce, the female starfish releases millions of microscopic eggs. Young starfish larvae eat plankton.

The crown-of-thorns starfish is covered with large, poisonous spines, which it uses to protect itself. This starfish eats coral polyps. Huge numbers of these starfish have been known to eat an entire coral reef!

Other varieties of starfish include the mottled star and the red blood star. The deadly sunflower starfish preys on other starfish.

The starfish family also includes sea lilies, feather stars, brittle stars, sea urchins, and sea cucumbers.

Sea urchins and sea cucumbers

⭐ **Sea urchins** are small creatures with spherical shells. Like starfish, sea urchins also have spines on their bodies.

⭐ **A sea urchin's spines** are movable and are used for defense and movement. They can be tiny or, in some cases, over 8 inches long.

⭐ **Certain fish**, like the triggerfish and the puffer fish, can knock off the sea urchin's spines with their hard heads.

⭐ **Sea urchins** eat small plants and animals. Some eat sponges.

⭐ **Some sea urchins** are venomous, and like certain jellyfish and stinging corals, they can be dangerous to divers.

⭐ **Sea cucumbers** are relatives of sea urchins and are found on seabeds across the world. They vary from 1 inch to 6 feet in length.

DID YOU KNOW?
The sea urchin's mouth is located on the bottom side of the test, or outer shell. Five teeth, moved by 60 muscles, help the urchin scrape food off the seabed. This jawlike apparatus is called an Aristotle's lantern.

⭐ **Sea cucumbers** get their name from their warty, tubular appearance. Unlike sea urchins, sea cucumbers have soft bodies. However, their skin is tough and leathery.

⭐ **The mouth** is located at one end of the body and is surrounded by tentacles that collect food. The diet of the sea cucumber consists mainly of small plants.

⭐ **Sea cucumbers** have tube feet and move about very slowly on the seabed by contracting their body. Some deep-sea varieties can swim.

⭐ **People hunt** sea cucumbers extensively. Also known as *trepang* in certain parts of Asia, dried sea cucumbers are used in soup.

▼ *This pencil urchin is a primitive, or cidarid, sea urchin.*

99

Sea snails and sea slugs

★ **Sea snails** are small, soft-bodied animals. They live inside coiled shells and move very slowly. Snails belong to the class Gastropoda, which means "belly-footed animals."

★ **There are over 50,000 kinds** of sea snails. These include whelks, limpets, top shells, winkles, cowries, and cone shells.

★ **Some sea snails** live along the coast, in rock pools and shallow water, while others live on the ocean floor. Unlike land snails, sea snails are very colorful.

▼ The yellow-spotted sea slug is one of the rarest species of sea slugs. Its brilliant red body, covered with bright yellow spots, is hard to miss.

► Cone shells use their long proboscis to shoot a poisonous dart into their prey. The venom is very powerful and quickly paralyzes the prey.

★ **Sea snails swim** or float along with the ocean currents. They use their muscular foot, or lower part of the body, for crawling over the seabed.

★ **Most sea snails** have four tentacles on their head. One pair helps them to feel their way around, while the other often has eyes at the tip. Some species do not have eyes at all.

★ **These creatures** have a tonguelike organ called the radula that consists of numerous tiny teeth. Some sea snails use the radula to pierce the shells of small animals.

★ **Like sea snails**, sea slugs also have a soft and slimy body. However, their body is not enclosed in a hard shell.

★ **Most sea slugs** have tentacles to sense prey. They eat algae, small snails, and sea anemones. Some of them also feed off corals.

★ **They are very colorful creatures**. Because they do not have a shell, sea slugs have developed various forms of defense. Some feed on poisonous sponges and develop toxins of their own.

★ **Some sea slugs** have long, hairlike tentacles on their backs. These tentacles often carry stings or fluids that taste foul. Certain species feed on corals to acquire their color patterns. This helps them blend in with their surroundings.

Mussels

★ **Several species** of freshwater and marine mussels are found around the world. They are usually wedge-shaped or pear-shaped and are 2–6 inches long.

★ **Mussels** are known as bivalves because they have two shells enclosing their soft, delicate body. Others in this group include oysters, clams, scallops, and cockles.

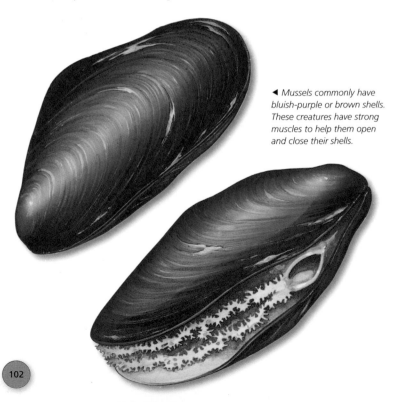

◄ *Mussels commonly have bluish-purple or brown shells. These creatures have strong muscles to help them open and close their shells.*

⭐ **These creatures** breathe with the help of gills. The gills have hairlike filaments, called cilia, over which water passes. The cilia are also used to capture food.

⭐ **Mussels are filter feeders** that feed on planktonic plants and animals. In some areas, mussels are so plentiful that this filtering action actually clears the normally turbid water.

⭐ **Most mussels** have a strong, muscular, tongue-shaped foot that extends from their body and sometimes remains outside their shells. They use this foot to dig.

⭐ **Toward the end** of the foot lies the byssus gland, or pit, which produces a tough thread. The mussel uses this thread to attach itself to various surfaces, such as rocks.

⭐ **Mussels** are known to defend themselves by tying down predators, such as snails, with their byssus threads.

⭐ **Some mussels** also use their hard shells to dig. They can drill holes into the wooden planks of ships.

⭐ **Mussels** often attach themselves to one another and form colonies or beds. Such formations are very common in the Wadden Sea, off the coast of Denmark.

⭐ **Pearls are obtained** from certain species of mussels. Those from the pinctada pearl oysters are considered among the most valuable.

Clams

★ **Clams are soft-bodied** animals. They belong to the same group as mussels, the bivalves, and are found across the world.

★ **Like other bivalves**, clams have two shells covering their body. Some clams can close their shells tightly when in danger.

★ **Clams have a single muscular foot** that enables them to dig. They use this foot to burrow into the sand.

★ **Most clams** are small in size, but the giant clam can be over 5 feet long. Giant clams are common in the depths of the Pacific Ocean, especially among coral reefs.

★ **The largest pearl** in the world was found in a giant clamshell. It was about 4.7 inches in diameter.

★ **Geoducks** are another variety of clams. They can be over 8 inches in length. They burrow deep into the sand and extend a long siphon to collect food.

★ **Unlike geoducks**, hard-shell clams do not burrow very deep. They are also called northern quahogs and are found to the north of the Atlantic Ocean. Southern quahogs have bigger shells than their northern counterparts.

★ **Razor clams** have thin and elongated shells that resemble a razor. They are found near sandy beaches and are very fast diggers.

★ **Soft-shell clams** are also known as steamer clams. They have long, brittle shells that do not cover their entire body—their neck hangs out from the shell.

⭐ **Clams are eaten** across the world and are, therefore, fished extensively. Clam farms have been set up in several countries, and these help to protect the natural populations.

▼ *A giant clam may grow to more than 5 feet in length and weigh as much as 500 pounds.*

Squid and cuttlefish

Squid are soft-bodied animals. Like cuttlefish and octopuses, squid belong to a group of mollusks called cephalopods. All of them are fierce predators.

All squid have ten tentacles, or arms, two of which are long and slender. All the tentacles have suckers at the ends. They are used to grab prey.

▲ A squid has a streamlined shape for swimming fast through the water.

These creatures can swim very fast. They move by releasing jets of water through a fleshy tube called a siphon, located near the head.

When in danger, squids shoot out a cloud of dark, inklike liquid. This hinders the attacker's vision, allowing the squid to escape.

The diet of a squid includes fish, crabs, and shrimps, as well as smaller squid. Predators of squid include whales, sharks, and big fish. Squid is also a popular food for humans.

The giant squid is not only the biggest of all squid, it is also the largest animal without a backbone. Its eyes, which measure more than 15 inches across, are also the largest among all animals.

Cuttlefish look like small, flattened squid. They have a fin that runs around the entire length of the body.

★ **Like squid**, cuttlefish also have ten tentacles, eight of which are small. Cuttlefish move in the same way as squid, releasing jets of water for short bursts of speed.

★ **The skin** of cuttlefish has tiny spots of various colors. Cuttlefish can control the size of these spots by using special muscles.

★ **Cuttlefish** have a bone called the cuttlebone, which is rich in calcium. It is sold in pet shops as bird food. In some parts of the world, people eat cuttlefish.

▼ *Cuttlefish are also known as "chameleons of the sea," due to their ability to change color according to their surroundings.*

Octopuses

★ **Octopuses belong** to the class Cephalopoda, which includes squid and cuttlefish. They have soft, sacklike bodies and large eyes that can distinguish colors.

★ **These marine creatures** vary in size. Most octopuses measure about 3 feet long. The giant octopus, however, grows over 23 feet in length.

★ **The most striking feature** of the octopus is its eight arms, or tentacles. Each tentacle has two rows of suckers, which help the octopus to hold its prey and also to climb rocks.

★ **Octopuses** use their arms to seize prey and pull it toward their mouth. They secrete poisonous saliva to paralyze the prey, and chew it using their jaws.

★ **The main diet** of the octopus consists of crabs and lobsters. Some species feed on small shellfish and plankton. They are, in turn, eaten by moray eels and sharks.

★ **Octopuses are considered** to be the most intelligent invertebrates, or animals without a backbone. They can recognize various shapes and are known to have a good memory. They can even figure out how to open a jar.

DID YOU KNOW?
Octopuses have a well-developed brain and the most advanced nervous system among invertebrates. Their nerve fibers are about 50 times thicker than human nerve fibers.

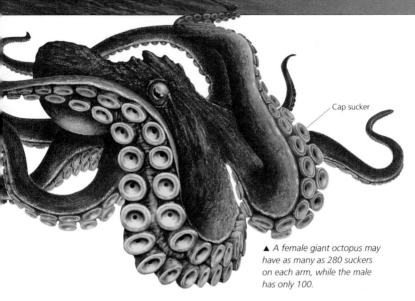

Cap sucker

▲ *A female giant octopus may have as many as 280 suckers on each arm, while the male has only 100.*

★ **These creatures** are largely bottom-dwellers and live in small coves. They create a pile of debris in front of their hiding nook to protect themselves. The Atlantic pygmy octopus lives in clamshells.

★ **The octopus can change** color quickly to camouflage itself. Some species produce fake eyespots when alarmed, while others use colors and lights to lure prey.

★ **Like squid**, some octopuses produce a dark, inklike fluid when in danger. Apart from clouding the predator's vision, the fluid is also believed to paralyze it.

★ **The blue-ringed octopus**, found in the Indian and Pacific oceans, has a very poisonous bite. When threatened, the blue rings on its body glow brightly to warn the predator.

Crabs

The oceans are home to a group of joint-limbed creatures, or arthropods, called crustaceans. This group includes crabs, lobsters, shrimps, and barnacles.

Crabs are the best known of all crustaceans. They have a flat body covered by a hard shell. There are over 5,000 species of crabs.

Most crabs live in the sea, but a few species can be found in freshwater. The common shore crab can live in both salt water and freshwater. It can even stay out of water for a few hours.

DID YOU KNOW?
The Japanese giant spider crab is the largest of all crabs. It can measure over 11 feet across its outstretched limbs. It is commonly found in the northern Pacific Ocean.

Crabs have five pairs of limbs. One pair of large, clawlike limbs, called pincers, is used for grabbing prey. The rest of the limbs are used to move around.

A crab also uses its pincers to defend itself. It digs a hole with the pincers and buries itself under the sand to hide from predators.

Crabs have highly specialized gills that do not clog even when they stay in muddy waters.

Unlike other crustaceans, crabs can move sideways. Due to their peculiar body shape, it is easier for crabs to escape into their burrows this way.

Large fish, otters, and octopuses are the crab's main enemies. These predators are able to break the shell easily.

⭐ **Some crabs** enlist the help of other creatures to protect themselves. The porcelain crab lives among the poisonous tentacles of sea anemones. This tiny crab also feeds on the anemone's leftovers.

⭐ **Certain crabs**, such as boxer crabs, grab hold of sea anemones with their pincers and wave them around to scare away their enemies.

▼ *Crabs are decapods—they have ten legs. The first pair are often strong pincers, used to tear up food.*

Hermit crabs

⭐ **The hermit crab** is very different from other crabs. It has a long, twisted abdomen, which lacks a protective shell.

⭐ **Most of a hermit crab's** important organs, such as the liver, are contained in the abdomen. The crab protects its soft abdomen by pushing it into the abandoned shells of certain sea snails, such as whelks.

⭐ **The hermit crab** carries its shell around. It holds it from the inside with two pairs of small rear legs. When in danger, the crab withdraws deep into this shell.

⭐ **Normally** the hermit crab has only one large pincer, because the shell cannot accommodate two. While hiding from its enemies, the crab uses this pincer to guard the entrance of the shell.

⭐ **As they grow in size**, hermit crabs start searching for bigger shells. They often fight among themselves to occupy a shell that suits their size.

DID YOU KNOW?
Robber crabs get their name from the fact that they are easily attracted to shiny materials. They have been known to steal pots and pans from houses and tents.

⭐ **Sometimes the hermit crab** carries sponges and sea anemones on its shell to keep enemies away. When the crab moves into a new shell, it takes its protectors with it.

⭐ **Hermit crabs** have highly developed antennae. These are much longer than those of other crabs and hence more effective in finding food.

▲ *Hermit crabs protect their soft bodies in a borrowed shell.*

Robber crabs belong to the same family as hermit crabs but are slightly different. Only young robber crabs use snail shells to protect their abdomen. Adults have hardened abdomens that do not require protection.

The robber crab lives on land and cannot swim. However, it has modified gills that need to be kept moist. The crab does this by dipping its legs in water and stroking them over the spongy tissues near the gills.

Robber crabs dig into the sand and hide during the day. They are excellent tree climbers. They are also known as coconut crabs, because they can break open coconuts with their powerful pincers.

113

Lobsters

★ **Lobsters** belong to the same group as crabs. Unlike crabs, these crustaceans have elongated bodies. They are often confused with crayfish, which are smaller.

★ **Lobsters have big heads** and their bodies are covered by a shell. They have five pairs of legs, one or more pairs of which are modified into pincers.

★ **In some species**, such as the American lobster, the pincers are enlarged and clawlike. One pincer is usually heavier and is used to crush, while the smaller one is used to cut and tear.

★ **American lobsters** are found near the west coast of the Atlantic Ocean, from Canada to North Carolina. They are extremely common near Maine and hence are more popularly known as Maine lobsters.

★ **Lobsters** have two pairs of antennae on their heads. The larger pair can be longer than the lobster's body. The lobster uses its antennae to feel its way around and to find food.

★ **The stomach** of the lobster contains toothlike grinding surfaces. The food is actually chewed within the stomach, which is located very close to the lobster's mouth.

★ **A fan-shaped tail** helps the lobster swim. It is believed that this tail also allows it to swim backward at high speed.

★ **When grabbed** by a predator, lobsters can discard their limbs and antennae to escape. Later, these lost parts grow back.

★ **Spiny lobsters** do not possess huge claws. Instead, their shells are covered with spines. This species can live for as long as 50 years.

★ **Most lobsters** live on the ocean floor, where they can hide by slipping into the spaces between rocks. They mostly feed on the remains of dead creatures. Lobsters also eat clams, snails, worms, and sea urchins.

◄ *Spiny lobsters are often seen migrating from shallow to deeper waters in groups of hundreds, or even thousands. Their movement in a single line is popularly known as "the march of the spinys."*

Shrimps and prawns

⭐ **Shrimps and prawns** are very similar in appearance. Both look like miniature lobsters. A hardened shell also covers their bodies, but this shell is not as thick or hard as that of lobsters.

⭐ **Shrimps have bodies** that are flattened from top to bottom, while the body of a prawn is flattened from either side.

⭐ **Prawns swim** using five pairs of paddlelike limbs located on their abdomen, while shrimps crawl around the seabed.

⭐ **Most shrimps and prawns** are almost transparent. This helps them hide from enemies. They turn pink only when cooked.

⭐ **Shrimps need** to shed their hard outer covering as they grow. At such times, most shrimps go into hiding.

⭐ **Both shrimps and prawns** are scavengers. They feed on almost anything, including dead marine animals.

▼ Prawns use their small pincers to search through the sand for food.

▲ *The spotted cleaner shrimp not only cleans the tentacles of the sea anemone, it also attracts other creatures for the anemone to prey on.*

Certain species, such as scarlet and skunk cleaner shrimps, live on coral reefs.

These brightly colored shrimps clean larger fish by picking tiny parasites off their bodies. The bigger predators therefore rarely harm cleaner shrimps. These shrimps even enter the mouths of the larger fish without being eaten.

Krill are small, shrimplike creatures that are found in cool oceans. They are the favorite food of some whales and sharks.

Millions of krill swim together in swarms that can be several miles long.

Barnacles

★ **Barnacles** are tiny crustaceans found in oceans, seas, and lakes. Their bodies are covered with a hard shell made up of platelike structures. The number of plates varies from species to species.

★ **Most barnacles** are around 0.5–1 inch across. However, the diadem whale barnacle grows to 2.5 inches. This species attaches itself to whales.

★ **Their long, featherlike limbs**, or cirri, help barnacles to trap tiny food particles. They mainly feed on plankton.

★ **Apart from rocks**, seaweeds, reefs, driftwood, and ships, barnacles also attach themselves to the bodies of whales, turtles, and other marine animals.

★ **Some barnacles** are tiny, parasitic organisms. They attach themselves to creatures such as crabs and feed off them.

★ **Acorn barnacles** use their plates to hold on to a surface. They are commonly seen on rocks along the seashore and in shallow water.

★ **In addition** to their shell-like plates, goose barnacles have muscular, stalklike structures. These help the creatures to attach themselves to floating objects, such as driftwood.

★ **Whelks are the most common** predators of barnacles. They can drill a hole through the barnacle's shell and eat the flesh inside. Mussels also feed on barnacles.

★ **Barnacles** often attach themselves to the bottoms of ships, thus increasing fuel consumption. A lot of time and money is spent removing them from hulls.

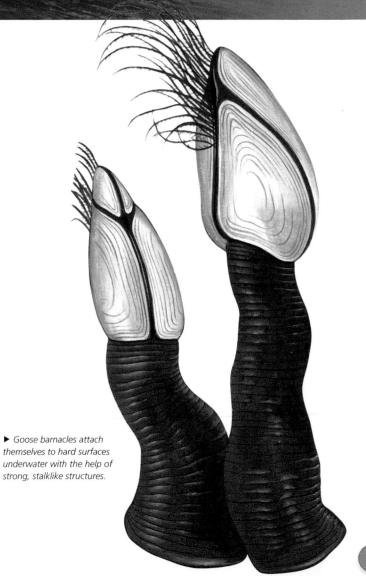

▶ Goose barnacles attach
themselves to hard surfaces
underwater with the help of
strong, stalklike structures.

119

What is a fish?

⭐ **Fish are vertebrates**, which means they have a backbone. They live in water, breathe through gills, and most have scaly bodies.

⭐ **There are more species** of fish than all mammals, reptiles, amphibians, and birds put together. Fish are found in varied habitats, from the deepest oceans to the smallest mountain streams. Most fish live in oceans and just one in five lives in freshwater.

▼ Inside a manta ray's mouth are five pairs of gill arches, which filter food from the water. The food particles get trapped, while the water passes out through the ray's gill slits.

★ **Unlike mammals,** fish are cold-blooded. Their body temperature changes with their surroundings.

★ **Fish are broadly divided** into two main groups—jawed and jawless. Jawless fish, such as lamprey and hagfish, have a suckerlike mouth with horny teeth.

★ **Jawed fish** can be further divided into cartilaginous and bony fish. The skeleton of cartilaginous fish is made up of a strong but flexible tissue called cartilage. Sharks, rays, and chimeras are cartilaginous fish.

★ **Bony fish** are the most abundant of all fish species. Their skeleton is made up of bones. Most of them have a bladder that helps them swim.

★ **Most fish** have a streamlined body that enables them to swim better. The sailfish and blue shark are among the fastest-swimming fish.

★ **Fish feed** on other creatures of the ocean. The smallest of fish feed on microscopic creatures such as zooplankton. Larger fish prey on smaller marine creatures.

★ **Fish are very important** to humans as food, since they are a good source of protein. Excessive fishing has endangered some species, while others are already extinct.

Anglerfish and cod

⭐ **Anglerfish** have a huge head and mouth. They also have numerous sharp teeth to trap their prey.

⭐ **Some anglerfish** are only 20 inches in length, while others could grow up to 6.5 feet. These are deep-sea fish found mainly in the Atlantic Ocean.

⭐ **Anglerfish** are normally dark brown or red in color. Their color gives them good camouflage.

⭐ **The diet** of anglerfish includes small cod, sprats, and dogfish.

⭐ **Some female deep-sea anglerfish** can eat prey bigger than themselves.

⭐ **Male deep-sea anglerfish** are much smaller than the female. The male attaches itself to the female with its teeth and extracts food from her bloodstream.

▶ Anglerfish are black or brown for camouflage. Only their glowing "fishing rod" is visible in the gloom.

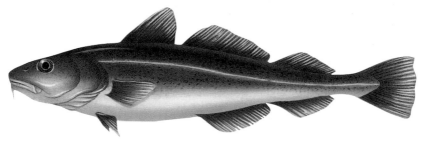

▲ *Cod have long, narrow bodies. They can grow to over 5 feet in length.*

★ **The common name** for the genus of fish known as *Gadus* is cod. Sometimes the term "cod" is used to refer to a wide variety of fish that are not in this genus.

★ **Cod are mostly found** in cold or temperate waters. They prefer to live in the depths of the ocean close to the seabed and feed on other fish.

★ **There are three main species** of cod. They are the Atlantic, the Pacific, and the Greenland cod.

★ **Cod are fished** extensively by humans for food. Cod liver oil is a rich source of vitamins and minerals, so cod is a valuable food for humans.

DID YOU KNOW?

Anglerfish get their name from the way the female deep-sea anglerfish catches its prey. It uses a long, wormlike spine attached to its head to attract smaller fish, and then traps them in its mouth. The spine is luminous, with a glowing tip to attract prey.

Salmon and viperfish

⭐ **Salmon** have elongated bodies and are excellent swimmers. They are usually found in the cold oceans near the northern continents.

▼ *Salmon spend from two to six years in their home river, then head out to sea, where they grow up to 5 feet long.*

⭐ **The diet** of salmon consists of smaller fish and crabs. The Atlantic and Pacific salmon are the best-known varieties of salmon.

⭐ **Most saltwater salmon** migrate to freshwater to lay eggs. The young ones later swim into the sea and live there. These young salmon return to the place where they were born when it is their turn to lay eggs.

⭐ **The journey** from the sea to the river can be over 1,000 miles, is very tiring, especially for the Pacific salmon, which has to leap up several waterfalls on its way. By the time the fish reaches the river and lays its eggs, it is exhausted and often falls prey to eagles and bears. Most Pacific salmon die after they have spawned.

⭐ **Unlike the Pacific salmon**, the Atlantic salmon survives its ordeal to return to the sea. They are even known to repeat their journey from sea to river two or three times in their lifetime.

⭐ **The fierce-looking viperfish** has a very big head but a slender, snakelike body. It is usually around 20 inches in length.

⭐ **Viperfish** have long, curved teeth that look like a snake's fangs. The mouth is huge, yet it is not large enough to cover their teeth.

⭐ **Although they are scattered** across the globe, viperfish are found mostly in tropical waters. They live near the ocean floor, at depths varying from 1,500 to 8,000 feet.

⭐ **Viperfish** prefer to stay in the dark ocean depths, but at night they swim up toward the surface in search of food.

⭐ **"Glow spots"** on the body and dorsal fin of the viperfish emit light to attract small fish and other prey.

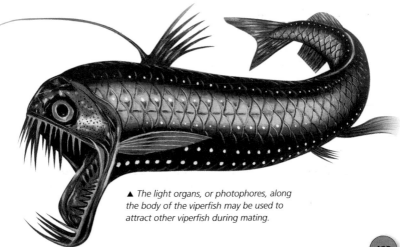

▲ *The light organs, or photophores, along the body of the viperfish may be used to attract other viperfish during mating.*

Flounder

- **Flounder have a unique shape**—they are flat and almost round. They belong to the group of fish known as flatfish.

- **Both eyes** of the flounder are located on the same side of the body—on the upper surface.

- **Some flounder** have both eyes on the left side, so they lie on their right side. Others have both eyes on the right side, so they lie on their left side.

- **These fish** prefer to live and swim close to the seabed. They are found in almost every ocean, but are more abundant in warm waters.

- **Flounder** undergo a dramatic transformation during their life cycle. The young are born looking like normal fish, but their body gradually becomes flatter and the eyes shift to either the left or the right side of the head.

- **The color of flounder** varies according to their habitat. They are usually brown, mottled, or sandy. The lower side of the body is often a lighter shade.

- **In addition to camouflage**, flounder have another interesting defense tactic. They cover themselves with dirt, leaving only their eyes still visible, so that predators cannot spot them.

★ **When attacked**, some flounder flap their fins on the seabed to stir up a cloud of silt that blocks them from the predator's view. They can then swim away to safety.

★ **Among the more common varieties** are the summer flounder, found in the Atlantic Ocean, and the winter flounder, also called the lemon sole, found in the south Atlantic and the Gulf of Mexico.

★ **Others in the flatfish family** include halibut, plaice, dab, turbot, brill, and windowpane flounder. The liver oil of the halibut, one of the largest flatfish, contains more vitamins than even cod liver oil.

◄ *The flounder's flattened shape and dull coloring help to camouflage it on the seabed.*

Grouper

⭐ **Grouper are large fish** that are found mainly in warm waters. They are abundant off the coasts of Australia and in the Caribbean Sea.

⭐ **They are characterized** by spines, or needlelike structures, near their dorsal fin. They have a large mouth and strong jaws. Most grouper, particularly the panther grouper, are marine predators.

⭐ **Grouper are strong swimmers**. They prefer to keep to the bottom of the sea or near coral reefs.

⭐ **The diet** of grouper includes crabs, cuttlefish, and other fish. Grouper use their strong jaws to kill prey and then swallow it whole.

⭐ **Grouper** are capable of changing their sex. Most grouper spawn as female for one or two years and change sex to function as males after that.

⭐ **These fish** can also change their body color. The red grouper changes its color according to the surroundings, while the blue-spotted grouper lightens its color when attacked.

⭐ **Grouper** are among the largest fish. Some species can grow larger than an adult human.

⭐ **The Australian grouper** and the jewfish, or spotted grouper, which can grow to over 10 feet, are the largest species. Some grouper can be as small as 4 inches.

⭐ **Small grouper** make fascinating aquarium fish because they have the ability to change color. However, some of them will eat their own kind.

⭐ **Nassau grouper** are extremely popular as food and are fished extensively.

▼ *Grouper wait patiently at the bottom of the sea and make small, swift movements to capture their prey.*

Triggerfish

⭐ **Triggerfish** are colorful fish found in shallow tropical waters. They grow up to 24 inches in length. They have strong jaws, sharp teeth, and eyes that are located on top of their head.

⭐ **These fish** have three dorsal spines. They use one of these as a trigger to lock or open the other two, giving it the name triggerfish.

⭐ **The triggerfish group** includes the puffer fish, the spiny porcupine fish and the ocean sunfish.

⭐ **The ocean sunfish** is shaped like a pancake and has thin dorsal and anal fins. Its tail fin is almost nonexistent, making the ocean sunfish a bad swimmer.

⭐ **Ocean sunfish** float on their sides on the surface of the water as if sunbathing. Hence the name sunfish.

◀ *Despite their huge size, sunfish feed on tiny plankton.*

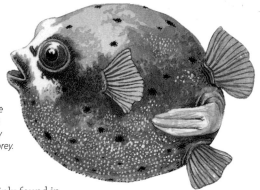

▶ *Most puffer fish have fused teeth that form a beaklike structure. They use this to crush their prey.*

★ **Puffer fish** are mainly found in tropical waters. Most of them are poisonous. The body of a puffer fish is round and covered with spines.

★ **The spines** of the puffer fish are usually not visible. But when attacked, the puffer fish swells its body, making the spines stand out. This is why they are also known as blowfish, globefish, and swellfish.

★ **The swelling** of the puffer fish is achieved by a sac inside its body, which it fills by gulping in air or water.

★ **Predators find** it tough to bite into puffer fish once they inflate themselves and their spines become erect.

★ **Puffer fish** is a popular delicacy in Japan. However, due to its poisonous nature, the fish can only be cooked by specially trained chefs. Chefs who have obtained a special license are allowed to prepare the dish.

DID YOU KNOW?
Ocean sunfish are among the biggest bony fish. They have a bulky, oval body and can grow up to 10 feet in length.

131

Snapper

⭐ **Snapper belong** to the same group as grouper and marlin. There are over 200 species of snapper.

⭐ **They are so called** because of their tendency to snap, or bite, swiftly at food.

▲ In a large group called a school, fish like these yellow snappers have less chance of being picked off by a predator.

- **Snapper are common** in tropical and subtropical waters of all oceans. Certain species of snapper also foray into freshwater in search of food.

- **These fish** have a slender body and a large, prominent mouth. Some species grow as long as 3 feet.

- **Snapper** are often found traveling in large schools. They eat small fish, mollusks, and other crustaceans. Some of them also eat plankton.

- **A well-known species** is the red snapper. It has a pinkish-red body with a lighter belly, and is commonly found in the Atlantic Ocean, especially along the western coast. Vermilion snapper are very similar to red snapper.

- **Emperor snapper** have black and white bands on their bodies. These bands, however, fade with age. They are among the larger snapper.

- **Dog snapper**, though fished for food, are sometimes toxic. They get their name from their prominent canine teeth, which make them look fierce.

- **Yellowtail snapper** have yellow spots and stripes. A prominent yellow stripe that begins at the mouth broadens gradually and runs to the tail. They are usually found in the Atlantic Ocean.

- **Blackfin snapper** are usually red with yellowish fins, and have a prominent comma-shaped mark at the base of their pectoral fins.

Flying fish

✳ **Flying fish do not actually fly**. Instead, they leap into the air and glide for short distances.

✳ **The average length** of a flying fish is around 8–12 inches. The California flying fish, found in the Pacific Ocean, is the largest species. It can grow up to a length of 16 inches.

✳ **The pectoral fins** of flying fish have similar functions to a bird's wings. The two-winged flying fish have very large pectoral fins that they stretch out to soar.

✳ **Some flying fish** have four "wings." In addition to large pectoral fins, these species also have large pelvic fins.

✳ **When threatened**, flying fish build up speed under the water's surface by thrashing their tails and holding their fins close to the body. The fish then leap into the air and glide for about 20–30 seconds.

✳ **Flying fish can leap** to a height of about 6 feet and cover a distance of over 500 feet. In between glides, the fish returns to the water to gain more speed.

✳ **They can glide** at double the speed they swim, and are known to accelerate from 22 mph in water to 45 mph in air.

⭐ **The ability of flying fish** to take off from the surface of the water and glide for some time helps them escape from sea predators like tuna and mackerel. But once in the air, they become the target of seabirds.

⭐ **Young flying fish** look very different from their parents. The young ones have whiskers on their lower jaw, which disappear when they mature.

⭐ **Flying fish** usually swim in schools. At times, a whole school leaps into the air and glides together.

▼ *Flying fish use their gliding ability effectively to escape from predators.*

Clown fish

* **Clown fish are also called** anemonefish. These fish live a sheltered life among the tentacles of sea anemones. They can grow up to 5 inches in length.

* **There are around 28 species** of clown fish. The most popular is the percula clown fish, which is bright orange in color with white bands.

* **Clown fish** are usually found in tropical waters. Since sea anemones are abundant in coral reefs, these fish can be found in the reefs of most oceans, the Red Sea, and around the Great Barrier Reef in Australia.

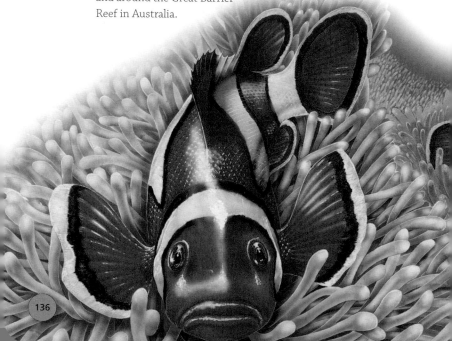

⭐ **Clown fish got their name** from the fact that their color resembles the costumes of circus clowns. Most of them are bright orange or red, with white bands.

⭐ **A unique relationship** exists between clown fish and sea anemones. The anemone protects the fish from predators, while the fish returns the favor by keeping its host's tentacles clean.

⭐ **The bright colors** of the clown fish lure other creatures to the anemone. Once the prey comes near, the anemone stings and feeds on it. The clown fish feeds on the anemone's leftovers.

⭐ **The close relationship** that exists between clown fish and sea anemones is called symbiosis. In such a relationship, neither animal can survive without the other.

⭐ **Clown fish** have a protective covering of mucus that keeps them safe from the tentacles of the sea anemones. This covering also prevents infections.

⭐ **It is believed** that a sea anemone can sense the presence of a clown fish because of certain chemical substances released by the fish. This prevents the anemone from stinging one when it comes close.

⭐ **Their bright colors** and playful nature make clown fish popular in aquariums.

◄ *Clown fish not only help clean the anemone but also eat its dead tentacles.*

Parrot fish

⭐ **Parrot fish are usually found** near coral reefs. They have a long body and a large head.

⭐ **These fish** are about 3 feet long. Some of them, such as the Indo-Pacific surf parrot fish, are much smaller, at around 18 inches.

▲ *There are different species of parrot fish. This spotlight parrot fish is very brightly colored.*

⭐ **The jaw teeth** of parrot fish are joined together to form a beaklike mouth. This beak is used to scrape algae and other food from coral reefs and rocks.

⭐ **When a parrot fish** scrapes off algae from coral reefs, bits of coral are also removed. Some of the coral bits are swallowed by the fish, to be excreted later in the form of silvery coral sand.

- **Parrot fish** also have grinding plates in their throat, with which they reduce food to a fine powder.

- **During the day**, parrot fish are active. At night, they sleep at the bottom of the reef. Some species even bury themselves in sand on the seabed and stay there until morning.

- **Sometimes parrot fish** surround themselves with a cocoon of mucus, or slime. Predators cannot detect the smell of the fish because of this mucus sac.

- **Parrot fish** rarely wander away from their coral home. However, during the mating season, they establish a breeding territory in the deeper waters surrounding the reefs.

- **Most parrot fish** are born as females, but as they become older, these fish transform into males. Some even change color when they change sex.

- **In Hawaii**, parrot fish are often eaten raw. However, they are more popular as ornamental fish.

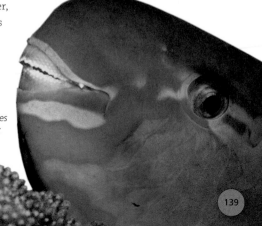

▶ A parrot fish snaps off pieces of coral with its beaklike front teeth and then crunches the coral with its back teeth.

Tuna and mackerel

⭐ **Tuna and mackerel** belong to the Scombridae family. Both of them are fast swimmers. Their torpedo-shaped bodies coupled with crescent tails give these fish enough power to thrust through the water at great speeds.

⭐ **Mackerel have** a sleek, shiny body and a large mouth. The head does not have any scales.

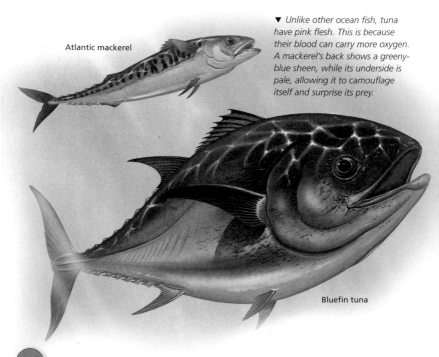

Atlantic mackerel

▼ *Unlike other ocean fish, tuna have pink flesh. This is because their blood can carry more oxygen. A mackerel's back shows a greeny-blue sheen, while its underside is pale, allowing it to camouflage itself and surprise its prey.*

Bluefin tuna

- **Huge schools of mackerel** can usually be found in cool waters off the coasts of the northeast United States, Canada, Great Britain, and Norway.

- **Mackerel** remain close to the water's surface and eat small crabs and fish.

- **The Atlantic mackerel** is the most common variety. It is blue and silver in color and can grow up to 20 inches long. Another equally well-known variety is the chub mackerel, found in the Pacific Ocean.

DID YOU KNOW?
Tuna was sold as a canned product for the first time in 1914. At the time, consumers thought that the meat tasted like chicken. Hence, the company that marketed canned tuna named their product "Chicken of the Sea."

- **Tuna are found** in most parts of the world. They have a rounded structure and are sleeker than mackerel.

- **Tuna** require a lot of oxygen. These fish swim with their mouth open, shooting jets of water over their gills. Oxygen is extracted from this water. Due to this system of breathing, tuna can never remain still.

- **Unlike most fish**, tuna are able to maintain a body temperature a few degrees warmer than the surrounding water. This is because of the extra oxygen carried by their blood.

- **Tuna swim** in schools and can travel long distances. They come to coastal areas to lay eggs. The eggs usually hatch within 24 hours.

- **Bluefin tuna** are large marine fish. Adults weigh over 1,500 pounds and can swim at a speed of about 55 mph.

Herring

⭐ **Herring are a family** of small, silvery marine fish that swim in large schools. They are often found in the temperate, shallow waters of the North Atlantic and the North Pacific.

⭐ **Herring feed** on small fish and plankton. They are an important part of the diet of larger creatures such as sharks, seals, whales, and seabirds.

⭐ **There are over 360 species** in the herring family, which includes fish such as sardines, anchovies, shad, menhaden, and sprats.

⭐ **Sardines** get their name from an island in the Mediterranean called Sardinia. The fish was once abundant near the coast of this island.

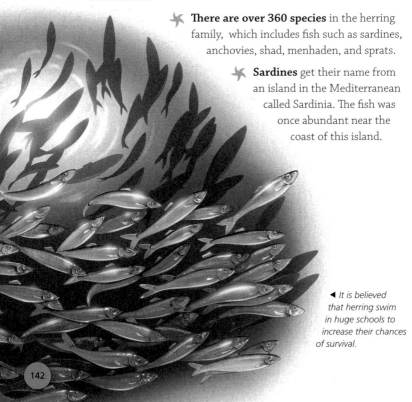

◄ *It is believed that herring swim in huge schools to increase their chances of survival.*

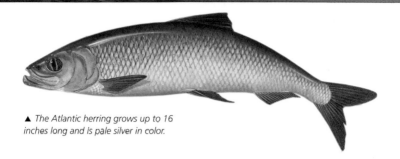

▲ The Atlantic herring grows up to 16 inches long and is pale silver in color.

⭐ **The name "sardine"** refers to various small fish canned with oil or sauce. In the United States, it is another name for herring. However, the true sardine is the young of the pilchard, found off the Mediterranean and Atlantic coasts.

⭐ **The body of herring** is streamlined, making them excellent swimmers. Most herring, sardines, and anchovies are less than 3 feet in length.

⭐ **The Atlantic herring** is the best-known variety and is believed to be the most abundant species of fish in the world.

⭐ **Atlantic herring** are bluish-green in color, with a silvery underside. The Pacific herring is quite similar to the Atlantic herring.

⭐ **The wolf herring** is the largest of the herring family. It is about 10 feet long and is a fierce hunter.

DID YOU KNOW?

The term "red herring," refering to a distraction, is derived from the processed version of the fish, which takes on reddish hues. It gives off a strong smell and was used during hunts to confuse the dogs.

⭐ **Herring are processed** and sold in several forms—smoked, dried, salted, or pickled.

Marlin

⭐ **Marlin are large sea fish**, closely related to swordfish, sailfish, and spearfish. Marlin and sailfish are also called billfish.

⭐ **Sailfish get their name** from their sail-like dorsal fin. Able to swim at a speed of over 60 mph, they are considered to be the fastest fish.

▶ *Marlin populations have reduced drastically in recent times due to sport fishing.*

White marlin

Blue marlin

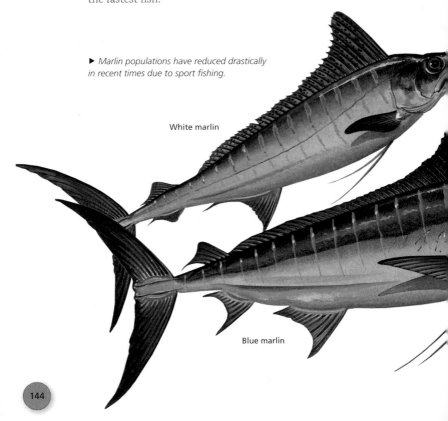

- **The dorsal fins** of marlin are smaller than those of the sailfish. Like sailfish and swordfish, marlin have snouts that are used for defense and attack.

- **The upper jaw** of marlin extends to form a long, rounded, spearlike snout. Marlin use this snout to capture food.

- **The diet** of marlin consists of squid, herring, mackerel, and crabs.

- **Marlin** are most abundant in the warm waters of the Atlantic and Pacific oceans.

- **Like sailfish**, marlin are fast swimmers and remain close to the ocean surface.

- **The blue marlin**, one of the largest species in the family, grows to a length of over 14 feet. It is found mainly in the Gulf Stream, in the North Atlantic Ocean.

- **The striped marlin** of the Pacific Ocean and the white marlin of the Atlantic are smaller varieties.

- **When caught**, marlin, particularly black marlin, leap into the air and fight vigorously to free themselves. This characteristic has made them popular game fish.

Swordfish

⭐ **Swordfish are found** in tropical and temperate waters. They are mostly dark in color, but have a lighter-colored belly.

⭐ **These fish** get their name from their upper jaw, which extends to form a long, swordlike snout with a sharp point. This jaw does not have teeth.

⭐ **The snout** is used for both defense and attack. It is believed that swordfish dash into schools of fish to injure or spear prey with their snout.

⭐ **Like marlin and sailfish**, swordfish are good swimmers. They can swim long distances in pursuit of prey.

⭐ **Fast swimmers**, swordfish have crescent-shaped tails, which are characteristic of belonging to the same family. However, unlike marlin, swordfish do not have pelvic fins.

▲ *Swordfish prefer to swim in water where ocean currents meet.*

* **Swordfish swim** near the surface of the water. Some species have been known to swim in schools, but most prefer to live alone.

* **Schools of small fish** such as mackerel and herring are the favorite food of swordfish. Sometimes they dive deep into the ocean in search of sardines.

* **Swordfish is a popular seafood**, eaten by many people around the world. Unfortunately, the swordfish population has decreased significantly because of overfishing.

* **When attacked**, swordfish can become very violent. It is believed that they can punch holes into small wooden boats. When they are wounded, they thrash about and can cause serious injury.

DID YOU KNOW?

Swordfish can grow over 13 feet in length. Their "sword" accounts for almost one-third of their length. The jaws of a young swordfish are equal in length. The upper jaw grows longer with age.

Barracuda

⭐ **In some coastal regions**, barracuda are more feared than sharks. They are powerful predators.

⭐ **Barracuda** are fierce-looking, with an elongated head and a long, slender body. Their length varies from 15 inches to almost 7 feet.

⭐ **These powerful swimmers** are found in the tropical waters of the Pacific, Atlantic, and Indian oceans.

⭐ **The mouth of the barracuda** contains a number of fanglike teeth. These predators have a forked tail and their dorsal fins are widely separated.

⭐ **The great barracuda**, found in the Pacific and Atlantic oceans, grows to a length of 6 feet and can be as heavy as 90 pounds. Also called the "tiger of the sea," this aggressive predator is known to attack divers and swimmers.

DID YOU KNOW?

Small barracudas are eaten by humans. However, if they feed on smaller fish that have eaten poisonous algae their flesh is also poisonous. The barracuda are themselves immune to this poison.

⭐ **The diet of barracuda** includes sardines, anchovies, and squid.

⭐ **Smaller barracuda**, especially those found in the Pacific Ocean, swim and hunt in schools. The larger ones lead a solitary life and hunt alone.

✴ **Barracuda** are often compared with sharks because of their aggressive nature. But unlike sharks, barracuda do not attack their prey repeatedly.

✴ **These fish** are guided by their sense of sight rather than smell. Divers avoid wearing bright colors that can attract these aggressive fish.

✴ **Their strength** and vigor have made barracuda extremely popular with anglers. Barracuda usually succeed in escaping from the fishhook, making the sport of game fishing more challenging.

◄ Barracuda are fearsome predators that seize, maim, and tear up other fish with their fanglike teeth.

Oarfish

⭐ **Oarfish** are so named because of their elongated, oar-shaped body. They are also known as ribbon fish.

⭐ **These fish** are deep-sea creatures and can be found in most oceans. They almost never come up to the surface of the sea.

⭐ **Live oarfish** have rarely been sighted by humans. People usually see them after they die and are washed ashore.

⭐ **Oarfish** have a bright red crest on the top of their head. This is the beginning of the dorsal fin, which stretches like a ribbon along the entire length of their silvery body.

⭐ **It is believed** that oarfish can raise and lower the crest on their head at will.

⭐ **Oarfish** are considered to be the longest bony fish in the world. They usually grow to around 20 feet in length, but some have been reported to reach over 50 feet.

DID YOU KNOW?

Oarfish have been the inspiraton for stories involving sea monsters. However, little is known about these mysterious deep-sea fish.

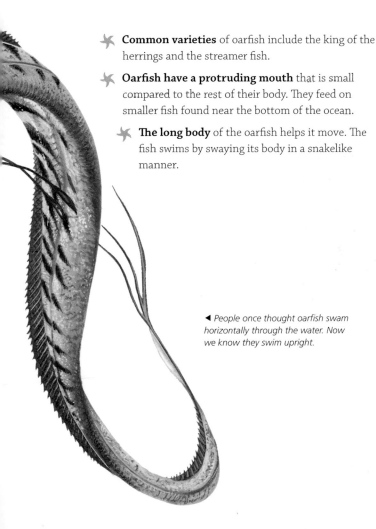

⭐ **Common varieties** of oarfish include the king of the herrings and the streamer fish.

⭐ **Oarfish have a protruding mouth** that is small compared to the rest of their body. They feed on smaller fish found near the bottom of the ocean.

⭐ **The long body** of the oarfish helps it move. The fish swims by swaying its body in a snakelike manner.

◀ *People once thought oarfish swam horizontally through the water. Now we know they swim upright.*

Eels

* **Eels are long**, slender, snakelike fish that live in shallow coastal waters around the world. Most eels live in the sea. However, a few are also found in freshwater.

* **Eels are normally** found among coral reefs and on the ocean floor. There are about 690 species of eels. The most common types include the conger, moray, and gulper eels.

* **Most species** of eels are around 3 feet long. However, the conger eel can grow up to 10 feet in length.

* **Eels do not have a tail fin**. Their dorsal fin, which runs along the top of the body, provides them with the power to swim.

* **Most eels** do not have scales on their body. Some species, however, have tiny scales. The body of most eels is covered with a slippery layer of mucus.

* **Some moray eels** can grow quite large. A species found in the Pacific Ocean has been known to grow over 11 feet in length. There are about 100 different species of moray eels.

* **Eels are graceful swimmers** but are not very fast. Some species, like the American eel, can breathe through their skin and can survive for some time out of water.

* **Gulper eels** live at a depth of almost 3,200 feet. Since light does not reach these parts of the ocean, they have very small eyes or none at all. These eels swim with their mouths open, ready to gulp down any creature that comes their way.

* **Freshwater eels** travel to the sea to lay eggs. The adults dive deep into the sea to breed and then die.

🌟 **The eggs of freshwater eels** hatch into leaf-shaped larvae that drift about for almost four years. Once they mature, the young eels, called elvers, swim back to the rivers, where they live until it is time for them to breed.

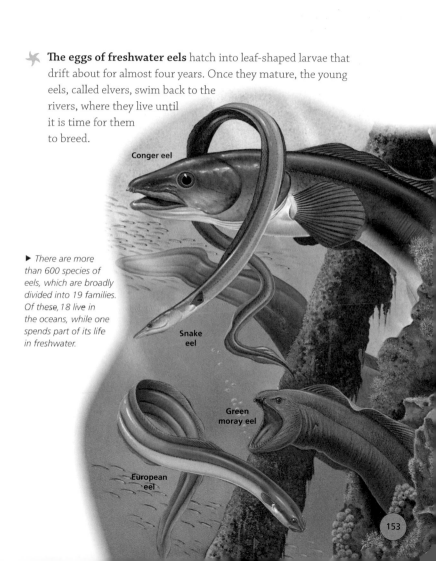

Conger eel

▶ *There are more than 600 species of eels, which are broadly divided into 19 families. Of these, 18 live in the oceans, while one spends part of its life in freshwater.*

Snake eel

Green moray eel

European eel

153

Sea horses

★ **Sea horses** are tiny ocean creatures that are very different from other fish in appearance. They get their name from their horse-shaped heads.

★ **The size** of a sea horse ranges from less than half an inch to about 5 inches. The common sea horse, found in the North Atlantic Ocean, is the largest species.

★ **Sea horses** have a long, snoutlike mouth with tubular jaws and an elongated tail. Their only similarity to fish is the dorsal fin.

★ **These creatures use** their curly tails to attach themselves to coral branches and seaweeds. They swim very slowly by flapping their dorsal fin.

★ **Sea horses live** close to seashores across the world. They eat small fish and plankton by swallowing them whole.

▶ *Sea horses exhibit beautiful, vibrant colors and are usually found swimming among coral reefs.*

⭐ **Instead of scales**, sea horses have a series of large, rectangular bony plates. These plates protect them from predators, such as crabs.

⭐ **The pencil-shaped pipefish** belongs to the same family as the sea horse. Like the sea horse, the pipefish has a long snout with no teeth. It can grow up to a length of about 20 inches.

⭐ **The sea horse family** consists of over 270 species. Sea dragons, shrimpfish, sea moths, and trumpetfish are in the same family.

⭐ **A female lays** eggs in a pouch on the male's body. The male carries the eggs while they hatch and until the young sea horses are able to swim out through an opening in the pouch.

⭐ **The Chinese** use sea horses to make traditional medicines. Sea horses are also valued as aquarium pets because of their unique shape and colors.

Rays

⭐ **Rays are cartilaginous fish**. Unlike bony fish, their skeletons are not made up of bones. Instead, they are made of a tough, elastic tissue called cartilage.

⭐ **Sharks and chimaeras**, or ratfish, belong to the same group of fish as rays.

▼ *The huge Atlantic manta ray has fleshy side flaps, or "horns," on its head that guide water into its mouth. It is shown here with two smaller types of rays.*

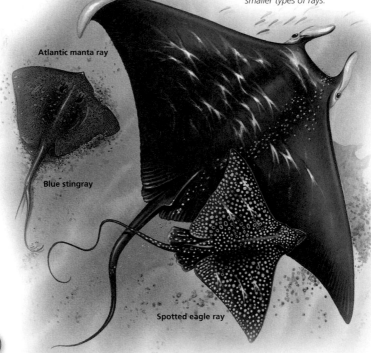

Atlantic manta ray

Blue stingray

Spotted eagle ray

- **Rays are found** in oceans across the world. Most rays live near the seabed. When in danger, they bury themselves in the sand.

- **These fish** have broad, flat bodies. Their eyes are located on the upper surface of the body, while the mouth and gills are on the lower side.

DID YOU KNOW?

The electric ray, also called the torpedo, has a pair of large electric organs between its head and pectoral fins. These organs can give powerful shocks measuring up to 200 volts. These shocks can stun or even kill prey.

- **Rays are usually brown** or black in color, but their underside is lighter. Certain species change their color to match their surroundings, which makes them hard to spot.

- **Some species** are less than 4 inches in width, while others measure over 20 feet across. Manta rays are the biggest of all rays.

- **The pectoral fins** of rays are located just behind their heads. These huge, winglike fins stretch from both sides of the head to the tail. The ray uses its "wings" to swim through the water.

- **Rays' tails** vary in size and structure. While most rays have a long tail, some have a short, broad one. Rays use their tail as a rudder while swimming and also to defend themselves.

- **Different species** of rays have different forms of defense. The long, whiplike tail of the stingray has one or more sharp spines that inject poison into prey.

- **Most species** of rays feed on crustaceans such as crabs, krill, and shrimps. The manta ray, however, prefers to eat plankton.

Sharks

⭐ **There are over 350 species** of sharks. They belong to the cartilaginous group of fish.

⭐ **Sharks** are found in oceans across the world. Some sharks, like the bull shark, can also survive in freshwater.

▲ The mako shark is slim and speedy, and races after prey such as mackerel, tuna, and squid. It can leap more than 30 feet out of the water.

★ **Most sharks** have torpedo-shaped bodies, which make them very good swimmers. They also have large tail fins that give them extra power for swimming.

★ **A shark's skin** is not covered with smooth scales like that of a bony fish. Instead, its skin is covered with tiny, toothlike structures called dermal denticles that give the skin a sandpaper-like quality.

★ **Sharks** are the primary predators of the ocean. They have special abilities that enable them to locate prey. The great white shark, the most feared predator of all, can smell a single drop of blood in 25 gallons of water.

★ **The whale shark** is the largest fish. It can grow up to 45 feet in length. However, some species, like the spined pygmy shark, are no more than 7 inches long.

★ **There are different shapes of sharks**. Hammerheads have a T-shaped head, which helps them make sharp turns. Reef-dwelling sharks have a flat body.

★ **The diet** of sharks includes seals, squids, fish, and other marine creatures. Some sharks, like the whale shark and the basking shark, eat plankton and small fish.

★ **Depending on their diet**, sharks have different kinds of teeth. Some, like the great white and tiger sharks, have sharp-pointed teeth that help them tear into their prey.

★ **Certain species**, like the reef sharks, have flat, platelike teeth that can crush the hard shells of the animals they eat.

Incredible hunters

Sharks are considered the best hunters in the ocean. These creatures have strong senses that help them hunt and travel great distances.

The most powerful weapon of a shark is its teeth. A shark can have as many as 3,000 teeth set in three rows. They rely on the first row of teeth to strike the initial blow. This first charge often injures or kills the prey.

Most sharks have a very good sense of smell. It is believed that almost one-third of the brain is devoted to detecting smell.

Some bottom-dwelling sharks have thick, whiskerlike projections on their snouts called nasal barbels. These organs help the shark to feel around for prey.

Sharks also have good eyesight. Most of them hunt at night and, like cats, have enhanced night vision. In clear water, sharks can spot their prey from a distance of 50 feet.

These fish do not have external ear flaps. Instead, their ears are inside their head, on either side of the brain case. Each ear leads to a small sensory pore in the shark's head.

It is believed that sharks can hear over a distance of 800 feet. They can detect sounds in the frequency of 25–100 hertz.

A pair of fluid-filled canals runs down either side of the shark's body, from its head to its tail. This is the lateral line, and it helps the fish sense minute vibrations in the water.

▲ *When great white sharks feel threatened, they open their mouths wide to show off sharp teeth.*

⭐ **The lateral line canals** are lined with tiny hairlike projections. These projections are triggered by even the slightest movement, which in turn alert the shark's brain.

⭐ **Most sharks** can detect weak electric currents released by other creatures. They do this with tiny pores located on their snout that lead to jelly-filled sacs called ampullae of Lorenzini.

Great white shark

★ **The great white shark** is the largest predatory shark. It has a pointed snout and a large tail fin. Great whites are commonly found in temperate to warm waters.

★ **The great white shark** is actually gray or bluish-gray in color, with a white underbelly. The great white is also known as "white pointer" and "white death."

▼ *The massive great white shark has been reported to have attacked boats, even sinking one near Nova Scotia, Canada.*

- **One of the biggest of all sharks**, the great white is normally about 15 feet in length. However, it is believed that some can grow as long as 20 feet.

- **Great white sharks** have around 3,000 sharp teeth with serrated, or sawlike, edges. The shark's teeth can grow up to 3 inches long.

- **The diet** of this shark includes sea lions, seals, and sea turtles. Young great whites eat fish, rays, and other, smaller sharks.

- **Great white sharks** do not chew their food. They use their sharp teeth to rip the prey into small pieces that are then swallowed whole.

- **The shark usually** approaches prey, such as seals, from below. Sometimes, while chasing seals, the shark leaps out of the water. This is called breaching.

- **Unlike other sharks**, great whites do not have a gas-filled swim bladder to keep them afloat. Therefore, they have to keep swimming to stay afloat.

- **The great white shark** does not lay eggs like other fish. The eggs remain inside the female's body until they hatch. The shark then gives birth to live young.

- **A surfer**, when viewed from below, looks very similar to a seal—the favorite food of the great white. Most biologists believe that this is the reason for great white attacks on surfers.

Tiger shark

⭐ **Tiger sharks** are dark gray in color, with an off-white belly. They get their name from the dark stripes on their back, which become lighter as the sharks grow older.

⭐ **The tiger shark** has a large, pointed tail fin. This provides it with the extra power that it needs to chase prey. The tiger shark also has a thick body and a blunt snout.

⭐ **Tiger sharks** are found in both tropical and temperate waters. They are most common in the Indian and Pacific oceans and the Caribbean Sea.

⭐ **The average length** of a tiger shark is about 10 feet. Some can grow as long as 20 feet. They are rarely attacked by other sharks because of their size.

⭐ **The mouth** of the tiger shark is large, with powerful jaws. The shark has three rows of curved, triangular teeth with sawlike edges.

▼ Tiger sharks leave their newborn pups to fend for themselves.

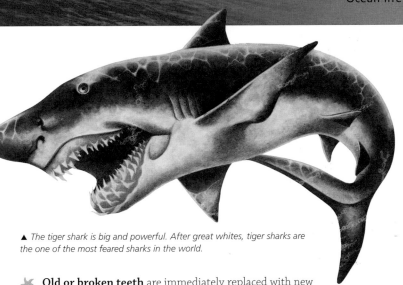

▲ *The tiger shark is big and powerful. After great whites, tiger sharks are the one of the most feared sharks in the world.*

Old or broken teeth are immediately replaced with new ones. It is believed that an average tiger shark can produce over 20,000 teeth in just ten years!

Tiger sharks are largely nocturnal and usually hunt at night. They have a good sense of smell and keen eyesight that aids them in hunting.

These sharks have excellent electroreceptors that can detect even the slightest movements in water. This helps them to locate prey even in dark, murky waters.

Tiger sharks eat almost anything—from fish and turtles to seals, seabirds, and other sharks. People have found tins cans, deer antlers, and even shoes in the stomachs of dead tiger sharks.

A slitlike opening behind each eye, called the spiracle, helps the tiger shark breathe. The spiracle passes oxygen directly to the eyes and brain, improving the shark's reflexes.

Hammerhead shark

⭐ **Hammerhead sharks** have a thick, wide, hammer-shaped head. Their eyes are located on either side of this T-shaped head.

⭐ **The head contains** tiny receptors that detect prey. Its unusual shape also helps the shark to take sharp turns.

⭐ **The hammerhead** is common in tropical and temperate waters. It is gray or brown in color, with an off-white belly. This shark migrates toward warmer waters near the equator in winter.

⭐ **The first dorsal fin** of the hammerhead, which is located on its back, is large and pointed. Like most sharks, it can be seen cutting through the water's surface as the hammerhead cruises along.

⭐ **The great hammerhead** is the largest in the hammerhead family. It can measure up to 13 feet in length. Bonnethead sharks are smaller and have a shovel-like head.

⭐ **Hammerhead sharks** normally feed on fish, smaller sharks, squid, and octopuses. Stingrays, however, are their favorite food.

⭐ **The great hammerhead** is an excellent hunter. It uses its highly developed senses of smell and direction to track prey.

⭐ **Large teeth** enable the great hammerhead to bite big chunks off its prey.

⭐ **Other varieties of hammerhead** sharks include the scalloped and the smooth hammerhead. Both types are found in moderately temperate waters.

⭐ **Most hammerheads** are harmless, but the great hammerhead is one of the few dangerous species. It is known to have attacked humans.

▼ *Hammerheads live in huge groups called schools.*
At night they separate and hunt alone.

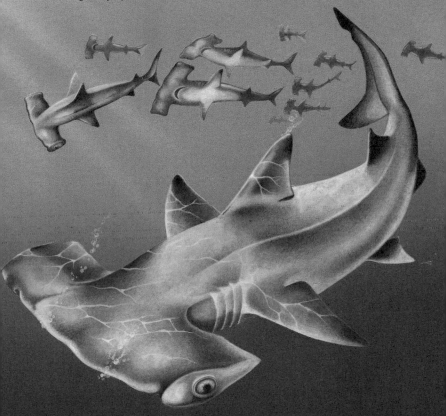

Blue shark

⭐ **The blue shark** is sleek with a long, pointed snout and large eyes. Its body is deep blue in color, with pale blue sides and a white belly.

⭐ **This shark** is also called the blue whaler because of its tendency to be present at the scenes of whale kills, to scavenge on the remains of dead whales.

⭐ **The blue shark** is one of the most abundant of all shark species. It prefers to live in the open sea and swim close to the surface. Blue sharks live in tropical, subtropical, and temperate waters.

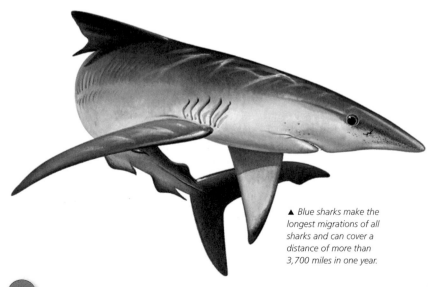

▲ Blue sharks make the longest migrations of all sharks and can cover a distance of more than 3,700 miles in one year.

- **The average length** of a blue shark is nearly 10 feet. The largest ones can grow to 12 feet.

- **A streamlined body** makes the blue shark the most graceful swimmer in the shark world. It has a long, pointed tail fin that gives it more power while swimming.

DID YOU KNOW?

When swimming at great speeds, the body temperature of blue sharks can rise almost 50°F above the temperature of the surrounding water.

- **Blue sharks** can reach speeds of 23 mph, making it one of the fastest sharks. In fact, it is second only to the mako in terms of speed.

- **The diet** of the blue shark includes small fish and squid. These sharks have long, saw-edged teeth, which help them grip squid and other slippery animals.

- **The blue shark** is one of the larger ocean predators. However, it is hunted by other sharks, such as the great white and shortfin mako.

- **Blue sharks** are not very aggressive. They are not considered harmful to humans, but they have been known to attack injured victims of air or sea disasters.

- **Blue sharks migrate** the longest distance of any shark, traveling across the Atlantic Ocean each year.

Thresher shark

★ **The thresher shark** is easily identified by its long, whiplike tail fin, which often exceeds the length of its body.

★ **Thresher sharks** can be found in tropical and cold-temperate waters around the world, but are most common in temperate waters. The common thresher is the most abundant species of them all.

★ **These sharks** are very shy and usually stay far away from the shore, but at times they swim close to the surface of coastal waters in search of food.

★ **The average length** of a thresher shark is 16 feet, but some species can grow up to 23 feet. It is dark blue or gray in color, with an off-white belly.

★ **Thresher sharks** are very good swimmers. Like all fast swimmers, they can maintain a higher body temperature than their surroundings.

★ **The thresher's** favorite food includes fish that swim in schools, such as herring, mackerel, bluefish, and butterfish. They are also known to eat squid.

★ **This shark** gets its name from the way it hunts. Since its teeth are smaller than those of other sharks, the thresher cannot use them to bite into its prey. Instead, it uses its tail to kill prey.

★ **The shark** first encircles schools of fish. It then stuns the prey by hitting it with its tail. Thresher sharks have also attacked seabirds with their long tails.

⭐ **Thresher sharks** hunt in groups or in pairs. They are nocturnal creatures, hunting at night.

⭐ **These sharks** are extremely shy and are considered harmless to humans. However, they have been known to attack boats. Apart from their meat and fins, thresher sharks are also fished for their hide and liver oil.

▼ *A thresher flicks its tail like an underwater whip, bashing small fish to stun or wound them. Then the thresher snaps them up in its mouth.*

171

Bull shark

⭐ **Bull sharks** are among the most feared fish in coastal regions. They get their name from their stocky build. They are heavy-bodied and have wide, blunt snouts.

⭐ **These sharks are** very aggressive and live in relatively shallow coastal waters. They have two dorsal fins and, as in all sharks, the first one is more pointed.

▼ *This bull shark is accompanied by a remora fish, which attaches itself to the shark. In return for ridding the shark's skin of parasites, the remora gets protection and scraps of food from its host.*

★ **These are the only sharks** that can be found in rivers and freshwater lakes. They have been reported to travel great distances upstream in warm rivers, such as the Mississippi and the Amazon.

DID YOU KNOW?

Most bull sharks are not migratory, but the South American bull shark travels thousands of miles from the Amazon River to the Atlantic Ocean.

★ **Bull sharks** are known by various names around the world. Some of these names are Ganges shark, Nicaragua shark, freshwater and Swan River whaler, Zambezi shark, and Van Rooyen's shark.

★ **On average**, bull sharks measure up to 6 feet in length. The females are much larger than the males.

★ **Bull sharks** are responsible for the most attacks on humans, after great whites and tiger sharks.

★ **The diet** of these sharks includes a wide variety of creatures. They eat rays, turtles, crabs, dolphins, seabirds, other sharks, and even dogs.

★ **Bull sharks** are not fast swimmers because of their bulk. However, they are capable of speeds of more than 12 mph in short bursts.

★ **Adult bull sharks** do not have natural enemies. But the young fall prey to larger sharks, including other bull sharks.

★ **These sharks** are rarely hunted for their meat. However, the hide is used to make leather products, while the fins are used to make shark-fin soup.

Lemon shark

✴ **Lemon sharks** are often confused with bull sharks because of their short snout. Like bull sharks, they are stocky and have big eyes.

✴ **These sharks** are found in the Atlantic and Pacific oceans and prefer to live in subtropical waters. They are found in abundance in the Caribbean Sea.

✴ **Lemon sharks** get their name from their color. The upper part of the body is deep yellow or yellowish-brown. The belly is either off-white or cream.

✴ **Most lemon sharks** are found near the shore. Sometimes they are even known to venture into river mouths, bays, and slightly salty or brackish waters, such as mangrove systems.

✴ **The average length** of a lemon shark is 7 feet. It can grow up to a maximum length of 10 feet.

✴ **Lemon sharks** feed on small sharks, crabs, shrimps, stingrays, and eagle rays. They have also been known to prey on seabirds.

✴ **These sharks** are bottom-dwelling creatures and can keep still near the seabed waiting for prey.

✴ **Their long**, thin, sharp teeth allow the lemon shark to easily bite into the flesh of slippery prey, such as squid.

✴ **Young lemon sharks** lose an entire set of teeth, one at a time, every seven to eight days. The lost teeth are replaced quickly.

✴ **Some people**, especially in China and Japan, eat lemon sharks. The fins are used to make shark-fin soup—a delicacy in China.

▼ Lemon sharks really are lemon in color. This helps to distinguish them from bull sharks, which are their close relatives.

Nurse shark

★ **Nurse sharks belong** to the carpet shark group. They are bottom-dwellers and hunt mainly at night.

★ **There are several theories** regarding the origins of the nurse shark's name. According to one, it was derived from the word *nusse*, a name that was used to describe cat sharks. Originally, the nurse shark was thought to belong to this group.

★ **Nurse sharks** have catlike whiskers on their jaws, which is why they were initially categorized in the cat shark group. In the Caribbean region, the shark is still called *tiburon gato*, meaning "cat shark."

★ **The catlike whiskers** of the nurse shark are called nasal barbels. These barbels are used for locating prey in the sand.

★ **Nurse sharks** can be found in tropical and subtropical waters in the Atlantic Ocean and eastern Pacific Ocean. They live mostly in coastal areas.

★ **The nurse shark** has a large, stout body, which is dark brown or gray in color. Its average length is 8 feet. Some can grow up to 13 feet.

★ **Nurse sharks** have small openings behind each eye. These openings, called spiracles, help the shark to breathe while eating or resting on the seabed.

DID YOU KNOW?

The nurse shark used to be hunted extensively. Its liver oil was used by sponge fishers to locate sponges on the ocean floor. It was believed that the oil could calm the water's surface, thus helping the fishermen to see clearly to the bottom.

✦ **During the day**, nurse sharks rest on the sandy seabed or in caves. They are known to live in the same shelter throughout their lifetime.

✦ **The nurse shark has a unique** way of feeding. It sucks in its prey at high speed.

✦ **The diet of the nurse shark** comprises fish and crustaceans such as shrimps and crabs. The shark has sharp teeth that are capable of crushing hard shells.

▲ *A diver creeps close to a nurse shark to get a closer look. The shark is hiding in a gap in a coral reef, a favorite habitat of nurse sharks.*

Reef shark

✴ **Reef sharks**, as their name suggests, live close to coral reefs. They are most common in the shallow tropical waters of the Indian and Pacific oceans.

✴ **There are three main** species of reef sharks. These are the blacktip, the whitetip, and the gray reef sharks.

✴ **Blacktip reef sharks** live in shallow waters. The tips of the fins are marked black and a white streak runs along their body. They have a blunt snout.

⭐ **These sharks feed** on squid, octopuses, and reef fish, such as millet. Blacktip reef sharks are often seen in groups.

⭐ **The average length** of a blacktip reef shark is 5 feet. Although they are not very large, they can become aggressive when disturbed.

⭐ **Whitetip reef sharks** have a body structure similar to that of blacktips. However, unlike blacktips, they have a white-tipped dorsal fin.

⭐ **Whitetips** have sharp teeth and feed on reef fish such as parrot fish, triggerfish, and eels.

⭐ **These sharks** are not as aggressive as other reef sharks. They spend most of their time resting at the bottom of the ocean.

⭐ **Gray reef sharks** are larger and more aggressive than the other two reef sharks. They can grow up to 8 feet in length. These sharks dwell in deeper waters.

⭐ **The diet** of a gray reef shark includes squid, octopuses, shrimps, and lobsters. Gray reef sharks are night hunters. During the day, they spend hours resting near the seabed.

◀ *Whitetip reef sharks sleep by day in caves or under rocks. At night, they go their separate ways and swim off to hunt.*

Port Jackson shark

★ **The Port Jackson** shark belongs to the family of horn sharks. All sharks in this family have hornlike spines on their dorsal fins, hence the name.

★ **Other species** in the horn shark family include Galápagos horn sharks, crested horn sharks, California horn sharks, and zebra horn sharks. Of the eight species of horn sharks, Port Jackson sharks are the best known.

★ **Port Jackson sharks** are most commonly found off the coast of Australia. They are usually gray in color, with brown or green tints. The upper part of the body has dark brown or black bands on it.

★ **These horn sharks** were named after Sydney Harbour, which was originally known as Port Jackson. The shark was first discovered in this area.

★ **Port Jackson sharks** are not very large and only grow to a length of 5.5 feet. They have a small, blunt snout.

★ **These sharks are bottom-dwelling** creatures and prefer to live near coral reefs or seaweed, where food is abundant.

★ **Port Jackson sharks** hunt at night. During the day, they rest in large numbers in sheltered areas like caves and reefs.

★ *Heterodontus*, the scientific name of the Port Jackson shark, means "different tooth." This shark has spiked front teeth, which it uses to hunt and hold its prey.

⭐ **Port Jackson sharks** eat reef-dwelling creatures such as crabs, oysters, and sea snails. Flat teeth plates at the rear of their jaws help them crush hard shells.

⭐ **These sharks** are also known as pigfish because of their blunt snout. In some parts of the world they are called oyster-crushers, as they can crush hard oyster shells.

▼ *The female Port Jackson shark lays about 10–16 corkscrew-shaped eggs, which she then wedges into crevices of rocks so that they are not washed away.*

181

Sawshark

🦈 **Sawsharks** have flat bodies and long, sawlike snouts lined with small, sharp teeth. The snout can measure up to one-third of the shark's body length.

🦈 **These sharks** live in warm and temperate waters around the world. They are abundant in the Gulf of Mexico and the coastal waters of the Indian Ocean.

🦈 **Sawsharks** normally keep close to the coastline and can even be found in lagoons, river mouths, and bays. They are bottom-dwellers.

🦈 **The average length** of a sawshark is less than 6.5 feet. Its body is blue or gray in color, with an off-white belly.

🦈 **Sawsharks** use their snout to injure prey. It is believed that these sharks move their heads from side to side, swiping at the prey.

🦈 **The sawshark's snout** is also used to dislodge hidden prey from the seabed. This shark eats small fish, squid, shrimps, crabs, and other crustaceans.

🦈 **Unlike the nurse shark**, the nasal barbels of the sawshark are located toward the tip of the snout instead of near the mouth. These barbels help the shark detect hidden prey.

🦈 **The sawlike snout** of a sawshark pup lacks sharp teeth and is covered with a protective membrane. This ensures that the mother is not injured during birth.

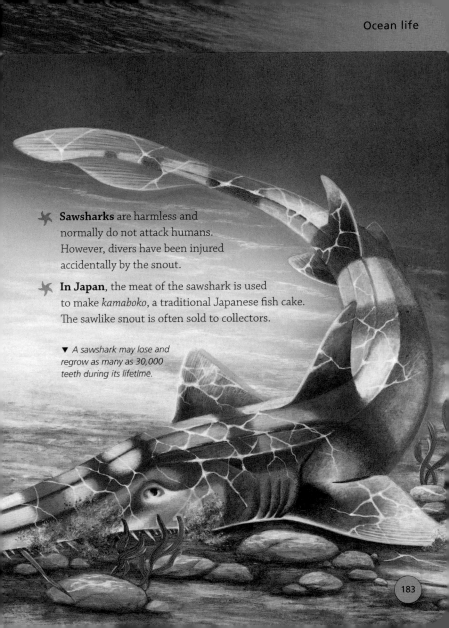

★ **Sawsharks** are harmless and normally do not attack humans. However, divers have been injured accidentally by the snout.

★ **In Japan**, the meat of the sawshark is used to make *kamaboko*, a traditional Japanese fish cake. The sawlike snout is often sold to collectors.

▼ *A sawshark may lose and regrow as many as 30,000 teeth during its lifetime.*

Sharks of the seabed

⭐ **Carpet sharks** are bottom-dwelling sharks. They have beautiful patterns on their skin that help them blend in with their surroundings. Most of these sharks are found near coral reefs.

⭐ **Wobbegong sharks**, nurse sharks, zebra sharks, bamboo sharks, and collared carpet sharks belong to this group.

⭐ **The whale shark** is another carpet shark. However, unlike its relatives, it is not a bottom-dweller.

⭐ **Some species**, such as bamboo sharks and collared carpet sharks, use their wide fins to "walk" on the seabed.

⭐ **The wobbegong** has a flat body and is very sluggish. It has fringes and tassels on its body that that make it look like rocks covered with seaweed. This shark waits motionless until the prey comes close and then grabs it.

⭐ **Like wobbegongs**, angel sharks are found near the seabed. Their large and winglike pectoral fins make angel sharks look very similar to rays.

⭐ **Angel sharks** are found in warm waters where food is abundant. Their size varies from 5–6.5 feet.

⭐ **Like wobbegongs**, angel sharks are also camouflage specialists. These sharks bury themselves in the sand. Only their eyes and a part of their head can be seen. When prey approaches, the shark lunges at it.

⭐ **Angel sharks** like to eat fish, crabs, lobsters, and squid. They are harmless to humans but can deliver a painful bite with their sharp teeth if disturbed.

★ **The eggs** of the angel shark are contained in a purselike casing that is commonly known as a mermaid's purse. The color of the eggs matches that of the surroundings.

▼ The wobbegong has green, yellow, or brown skin. This helps it hide among the rocks and seaweed on the seabed. It can grab any passing fish to eat.

Greenland sharks

* **Greenland sharks** are found in cold Arctic waters. They live in the region throughout the year. They prefer to feed in shallow waters during winter.

* **These sharks** are extremely lazy and are hence known as sleeper sharks. Greenland sharks are also called gurry sharks.

▼ *Although the Greenland shark prefers icy waters, some have been sighted off the coast of Maine.*

- **They are one** of the bigger shark species. Their average length is about 16 feet, but some of them can grow to over 20 feet. The largest recorded specimen was 21 feet long.

- **Greenland sharks** are grayish-brown and have small fins. The dorsal fin is smaller than in most other sharks. This helps them swim under sheets of ice. They have a rounded snout.

- **These sharks** feed on a wide variety of prey. Their diet includes fish, seals, squid, and dead whales. They use their short but sharp teeth to dig into the flesh of their prey.

- **Despite their sluggish nature**, they are known to hunt fast-swimming fish such as salmon. They are ambush hunters and wait until their prey is close enough before they attack.

- **Most Greenland sharks** have parasites called copepods clinging to their eyes. Until recently, it was believed that these copepods glow in dark waters and attract prey.

- **The meat** of the Greenland shark is poisonous and has to be dried or boiled thoroughly before consumption.

- **Greenland sharks' flesh** contains high concentrations of chemicals such as urea and trimethylamine oxide. These induce an alcoholic effect on those who eat the meat without cooking it properly. For this reason, the Greenlanders call people who are drunk "shark-sick."

- **Inuit hunt** Greenland sharks for their skin, which is used for making boots. The teeth of these sharks are used to make knives.

Whale shark

- **Whale sharks** are the largest fish in the world. They are not aggressive and pose no threat to humans.

- **Whale sharks prefer to live** in warm tropical waters and are found in many areas across the world. They are rarely found in temperate waters.

- **The average length** of a whale shark is about 46 feet. However, some have been known to grow to over 60 feet in length.

- **These gentle giants** are also very heavy. An average adult whale shark weighs about 15 tons. Owing to their size, these sharks cannot move fast. They swim by moving their enormous bodies from side to side.

- **Whale sharks** are dark gray or brown in color and their underside is off-white. They have white dots and lines on their backs.

- **The mouth** of the whale shark is extremely large and can be as wide as 4.5 feet. They have around 300 rows of tiny, hooklike teeth in each jaw.

- **These sharks** move about with their mouths open and suck in vast quantities of water rich in plankton. Special bristles attached to the gills filter the tiny prey, while the water is thrown out through the gill slits.

- **Whale sharks** have a huge appetite. They feed mainly on plankton, sardines, krill, and anchovies.

★ **These sharks** also love to eat fish eggs. They are known to wait for hours at breeding grounds to capture freshly laid eggs. They are even known to return to the same mating grounds year after year during the breeding season.

★ **Sometimes**, whale sharks can be seen swimming in schools. However, they usually travel alone.

▼ *The whale shark has patterns of light spots and stripes on a dark body. These help the shark to blend into its surroundings.*

Basking and megamouth sharks

⭐ **Basking sharks** are similar to whale sharks but slightly smaller. Their average length is around 33 feet, but some species grow up to 42 feet.

⭐ **Like whale sharks**, basking sharks have filters on their gills, which trap prey while they draw in water. These sharks also feed on plankton and small fish.

▲ *The megamouth shark is so different from other sharks that it was classified under its own, unique name—Megachasmidae.*

* **Basking sharks** are grayish-brown or black, with an off-white belly. Found in temperate coastal waters around the world, these sharks get their name from the fact that they spend most of their time at the surface of the water, appearing to "bask" in the sun.

* **Unlike whale sharks** that swim alone, basking sharks have been known to swim in schools of up to 100 fish.

* **Basking sharks** have more teeth than most sharks. Their gaping mouths can accommodate as many as 1,500 teeth!

* **The megamouth shark** gets its name from the fact that it has a large head and a huge mouth. This deepwater shark can be found in the Indian and Pacific oceans.

* **Thought to be less active**, megamouth sharks are even slower than basking sharks. It is believed that a flabby body and soft fins are responsible for its poor mobility.

* **The megamouth shark** was first discovered in 1976 and very few sightings of the shark have been reported since then.

* **Like basking sharks**, megamouths are also filter feeders. They come to the surface at night to feed on plankton.

* **The megamouth** is so rare that not much is known about its habits. However, like the basking shark, this species is harmless to humans.

Sea turtles

⋆ **There are only seven species** of marine turtles. They are found in tropical and subtropical waters around the world.

⋆ **The leatherback turtle** is the largest sea turtle. The other species are loggerhead, hawksbill, olive ridley, Kemp's ridley, flatback, and green sea turtles.

⋆ **A hard shell** covers and protects the sea turtle's body. Compared to the freshwater turtle, the sea turtle has a flatter, less-domed shell, which helps it swim faster.

▼ Sea turtles spend most of their lives in water. They swim swiftly by flapping their large, flipperlike front limbs.

- **The front limbs** of the sea turtle are larger than the back limbs. These flipperlike limbs help the turtle to "fly" through the water, although its movement on land is awkward.

DID YOU KNOW?

It is believed that sea turtles have been on our planet for over 100 million years. They have survived while other prehistoric animals, such as dinosaurs, have become extinct.

- **The shell** of the leatherback sea turtle is made of a thick, rubbery substance that is strengthened by small bones. These turtles are named after this unusual shell.

- **Sea snakes and sea turtles** are the only reptiles that spend most of their lives in the ocean. The females swim ashore for only a few hours each year to lay eggs.

- **Sea turtles** prefer to lay their eggs at night. The female digs a pit in the sand with her flippers. She then lays about 50–150 eggs, and covers the nest with sand.

- **Once the eggs hatch**, the young turtles struggle out of their sandpit and make their way to the sea. On the way, many babies fall prey to seabirds, crabs, otters, and other predators.

- **The diet of sea turtles** differs from species to species. Leatherbacks prefer jellyfish, while olive ridleys and loggerheads eat hard-shelled creatures such as crabs. Sponges are a favorite of hawksbills.

- **Most turtle species** are under threat because they are hunted for their eggs, meat, and shells. The trade in turtles has been declared illegal in most countries, but people continue to kill them.

Loggerhead turtle

★ **Loggerhead turtles** get their name for their unusually large heads. Compared to other sea turtles, their head is bigger than their body. The Scottish word *logger* means "block of wood," while *loggerhead* means "stupid" or "clumsy"!

★ **The upper shell** of loggerhead turtles averages over 3 feet in length. Adult loggerheads weigh more than 220 pounds.

★ **Most loggerheads** prefer temperate and subtropical waters. Some species inhabit muddy waters, but most live in clear seas.

★ **Like other sea turtles**, female loggerheads come ashore to build nests and lay their eggs. These nesting activities take place during the night.

★ **The heart-shaped shell**, or carapace, is bony and lacks any ridges. The front flippers of the turtle are short and thick, with two claws. The rear flippers have either two or three claws.

★ **Loggerheads' shells** are reddish-brown in color. The scales on top of the head and flippers are the same color, but with yellow borders. Loggerheads' shells have a paler, yellowish underside.

◄ *Loggerhead turtles have strong jaws with very sharp, horny edges.*

▼ Masirah Island, off the coast of Oman, supports the largest single nesting population of loggerhead turtles. It is home to as many as 30,000 nesting females each year. These young loggerheads have just hatched. Not all of them make it to the sea. As they race down the beach, some are picked off by hungry gulls or crabs.

* **Young loggerheads** are mostly light brown in color, with a dark brown shell. They are about 1.5 inches long and weigh less than an ounce.

* **Loggerheads** are carnivorous and have powerful jaws that can crush hard shells. They feed mainly on crabs, mussels, sea snails, lobsters, and clams. They are also known to eat jellyfish.

* **Like leatherback turtles**, loggerheads often mistake plastic bags for jellyfish and eat them. This often proves to be fatal.

* **Loggerheads** are an endangered species. A large number get caught and killed in fishing nets. Overcrowding on beaches has also led to a decline in nesting activities.

Hawksbill turtle

★ **Hawksbill turtles** get their name from their narrow, curved upper jaw that looks like a hawk's beak.

★ **These turtles** are not very large. On average, their upper shell is less than 3 feet in length. They have an elongated head and body, and claws on their flippers.

▲ *The hawksbill turtle has been listed as endangered since 1970.*

- **Hawksbill turtles** are black, gray, or brown in color. Their underside is light yellow or white, while their shell is orange, brown, or yellow.

- **Newly hatched turtles** are about 1.5 inches in length and weigh about 0.5 ounce.

- **These sea turtles** prefer tropical waters. They are commonly found among coral reefs in the tropical Atlantic, Pacific, and Indian oceans.

- **The shell** of a young hawksbill is heart-shaped. However, this becomes more elongated as the turtle grows older.

- **The turtle's narrow head** and beaklike jaws allow it to pick food from small openings in coral reefs. Although sponges form their main diet, hawksbills also feed on shrimps, squid, and anemones.

- **Like other sea turtles**, female hawksbills lay their eggs in sandpits. However, these turtles have very specific nesting areas, to which they return year after year.

- **In Japan**, the hawksbill's ornate shell was widely used to make richly crafted jewelry, such as brooches, necklaces, combs, hairpins, and other accessories. These turtles are, therefore, also called tortoiseshell turtles.

- **As with most sea turtles**, the population of the hawksbill is threatened. Apart from being killed for their shells, a large number of them die each year by getting caught in fishing nets.

Olive ridley turtle

⭐ **Olive ridley turtles** are one of the smallest sea turtles. They are named after the color of their olive-green shell. Some believe they were named after H. N. Ridley, a botanist who reportedly sighted the species first.

⭐ **The average length** of the olive ridley's shell is less than 27 inches. Although the shell is wide, it is not as wide as that of the closely related Kemp's ridley turtle.

⭐ **The front and rear flippers** of olive ridleys have one or two claws, but an extra claw is often seen on the front limbs. Like loggerheads, they have strong jaws.

⭐ **These turtles** are found in the warm waters of the Indian, Pacific, and Atlantic oceans. Most of them prefer shallow waters.

⭐ **Olive ridleys** are also called Pacific ridleys. They are distinguished from Kemp ridleys by their color and size.

⭐ **When the water gets too cold**, olive ridleys are known to bask in the sun in large groups. This helps them maintain their body temperature.

DID YOU KNOW?

Arribadas can be found on isolated beaches in the Bay of Bengal in India, and in Costa Rica and Mexico. These nesting groups, however, are unpredictable and could be caused by climatic conditions, such as strong offshore winds, or by certain moon or tide phases.

◀ Olive ridley turtles are also called Pacific ridley turtles. They are larger than their Atlantic counterparts, Kemp's ridley turtles.

⭐ **During the nesting season** a large number of females, sometimes thousands, come together on the same beach to lay eggs. These nesting groups are called *arribadas* or *arribazones* and are characteristic of olive ridleys.

⭐ **An olive ridley turtle** can nest more than once in a season, with an interval of 14 days in between.

⭐ **Olive ridleys** like to eat jellyfish, crabs, shrimps, sea urchins, and other small marine creatures. They also feed on algae.

⭐ **These turtles** are an endangered species, said to be near extinction. They build their nests on a select few beaches. Human activities on these beaches have led to destruction of their nests.

Green sea turtle

⭐ **Green sea turtles** get their name from the green color of the fat under their shell. These turtles have a small head that cannot be retracted into the shell.

⭐ **Black-brown or greenish-yellow** in color, the shell also has black markings. The underside is paler in color. It is smooth to the touch.

⭐ **The shell** can be up to 5 feet in length and has big plates on either side. Atlantic green turtles tend to be larger than their Hawaiian relatives.

▶ Female green sea turtles travel up to 1,800 miles to their breeding grounds to lay eggs.

★ **Newly hatched green sea turtles** are about 2 inches long and weigh almost 1 ounce. They are black in color, with white undersides.

★ **Green sea turtles** prefer the warm waters of the tropical and temperate seas. They are found in oceans across the world, and are often seen in shallow coastal waters.

★ **Hawaiian green sea turtles** come ashore and lie motionless in the sun for hours. They do this to rest and warm up.

★ **Adult green sea turtles** feed mainly on marine plants. However, the young also eat shrimps, jellyfish, and insects.

★ **People kill these turtles** for their eggs, shells, and meat. At one time the green sea turtle was extensively hunted for its calipee, which is a vital ingredient in turtle soup.

★ **Calipee is the cartilage** found under the bottom shell, or plastron, of the turtle. Poachers used to cut the calipee out and leave the turtle to bleed to death.

Leatherback turtle

Leatherback turtles are the biggest sea turtles, with an average length of about 6.5 feet. In some cases, a leatherback may grow to almost 10 feet. These turtles can weigh over 1,100 pounds.

The largest leatherback ever recorded was an adult male that was found stranded on the west coast of Wales in 1988. It weighed over 1,900 pounds.

Leatherbacks usually have a higher body temperature than the surrounding water. This is the reason leatherbacks can survive even in extremely cold places such as Greenland and Iceland.

The turtle's rubbery shell has prominent ridges that run along its length. The ridges make the shell look like a boat's hull. Leatherbacks floating on the surface of the water are, therefore, often mistaken for upturned boats.

The outer shell, or carapace, of the leatherback is either dark gray or black, with white spots. Newborn turtles have white blotches on their carapace.

These turtles have delicate, scissorlike jaws that are easily damaged. Consequently, they only eat soft-bodied creatures.

Leatherbacks feed almost exclusively on jellyfish, although some have been known to eat sea urchins and squid.

The food pipe, or esophagus, contains long spines that point backward. This allows the turtle to swallow jellyfish and other slippery food.

Many leatherbacks have reportedly died by eating floating plastic bags, which they mistake for jellyfish.

✳ **In 1982**, an estimated 115,000 adult female leatherbacks existed worldwide. These numbers have drastically declined in recent years, largely due to pollution and overfishing. Leatherbacks are often bycatches, caught accidentally in fishing nets.

▲ *Swimming to depths of over 3,000 feet, leatherback turtles dive deeper than any other sea turtle. They also migrate the farthest, traveling up to thousands of miles at a stretch.*

Sea snakes

⭐ **Sea snakes** are mainly found in the warm waters of the Indian and Pacific oceans. They can be ten times more venomous than most land snakes.

⭐ **These snakes feed on small fish**, eels, and fish eggs. Sea snakes use their strong venom to kill prey, and then swallow it whole.

⭐ **The scales** on a sea snake are small. This reduces friction, which helps the animal swim faster. The sea snake also has a flat, paddlelike tail that aids in swimming.

⭐ **Being reptiles**, sea snakes do not have gills. They have to come up to the surface of the water to breathe. However, they are able to absorb some oxygen from the water that they swallow. This helps them stay underwater for longer periods.

⭐ **The sea snake** has a special gland under its tongue that gets rid of excess salt from seawater. It also has highly developed nostril valves that can be closed while diving into the depths of the ocean.

⭐ **There are two kinds of sea snakes**. Aquatic sea snakes never leave the water, not even to breed, while amphibious sea snakes, or sea kraits, slither onto land to lay their eggs.

⭐ **Aquatic sea snakes**, or "true" sea snakes, are viviparous. This means that the female does not lay eggs, but gives birth to live young.

⭐ **The yellow-bellied sea snake** is the most easily recognized true sea snake. It is named for its bright yellow belly. Although this snake is extremely poisonous, it attacks only when disturbed.

⭐ **This sea snake** can swim backward and is the fastest swimmer among sea snakes, reaching a speed of 2.2 mph. It is also capable of staying underwater for three hours before coming up to the surface to breathe.

⭐ **Sea kraits** have colored bands on their body. Unlike true sea snakes, sea kraits have wide scales on their bellies that help them move on land.

▼ ▶ *Sea snakes use venom (poison) to stun prey. The venom of sea snakes is more powerful than that of any land snake.*

Banded sea snake

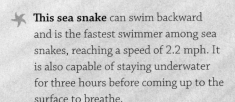

Yellow-bellied sea snake

205

Gulls

✳ **A large number** of birds live around the oceans. Of these, gulls, or seagulls, are the most common. These birds are migratory and there are about 43 species around the world.

✳ **Gulls** range in length from 11–31 inches. Most species have white and gray plumage, or feathers. Some have black markings on the back, wings, and head.

✳ **These birds** have a sharp, hooked bill, which helps them kill small birds and similar prey. They also have webbed feet to paddle on water surfaces. Gulls cannot dive underwater.

▼ These swallow-tailed gulls are found in the Galápagos islands and are the only gull with a deeply forked tail.

★ **Gulls** use the wind to stay aloft without flapping their wings.

★ **The color** of the plumage changes throughout the gull's life. Some even have a different winter and summer plumage.

★ **Black-headed gulls** have dark heads and red-colored bills in summer. In winter, however, the heads of these species turn white, with a dark gray spot. It is believed that this gives the bird better camouflage in the snow.

DID YOU KNOW?

Gulls might be popularly called seagulls, but very few species actually venture into the open seas. Most prefer to keep to the shore, while some come to the coast only during the breeding season.

★ **Many gulls** venture inland and hunt among garbage for food. They are also great scavengers and feed on dead animal matter along seashores.

★ **These birds** are able to fish in shallow waters and often prey on the eggs of other seabirds. Some of them even feed on eggs laid by their own species.

★ **Gulls make** simple grass-lined nests, mostly on flat ground in isolated areas of beaches. Some nest on ledges in cliffs.

★ **Commonly found** species include the herring, common, black-headed, and ring-billed gulls. The great black-backed gull is the largest of all.

Pelicans

* **Pelicans can be easily identified** by their long bill and massive throat pouch. They are strong swimmers and the largest diving birds.

* **These birds** have a long neck and short legs. Adult pelicans grow up to 6 feet in length and weigh 9–15 pounds. Males are larger than females. Their wingspan can measure up to 10 feet.

* **There are seven species** of pelicans. All are found in warmer climates. Most pelicans can also live near bodies of freshwater. The brown pelican, however, is excusively a seabird.

* **Most pelicans** are white, except for brown and Peruvian pelicans, which are dark in color. American white pelicans have black wing tips.

* **Pelicans** breed in colonies. Nearly 40,000 birds come together on isolated shores or islands to breed.

* **In some species**, the color of the bill and pouch changes during the mating season. The front part of the pouch turns a bright salmon-pink, while the base becomes deep yellow. Parts of the bill change to bright blue, and a black strip can be seen from the base to the tip.

* **The female pelican** builds a nest by digging a hole in the ground using her bill and feet. She then lines the hole with grass, leaves, and feathers. Three days later, she lays about three eggs in her new nest.

⭐ **While fishing**, this bird uses its pouch as a net to catch the prey. Once the prey is caught, the pelican draws the pouch close to its chest to empty the water out and swallow the prey. Food is also carried in the pouch and is later retrieved to feed the chicks.

⭐ **Different species** have different hunting techniques. Brown and Peruvian pelicans dive headfirst into the water to catch fish.

⭐ **Most other pelicans** swim and then pounce on their prey. Some fish in groups and drive the fish toward shallow waters, where it is easier to capture them. Pelicans feed on small fish and crustaceans.

▼ *Pelicans, such as this American white pelican, use their throat pouch like a net to catch fish.*

Albatrosses

★ **The albatross** is the largest seabird, weighing about 25 pounds. It is commonly found in oceans of the Southern Hemisphere, but some species also dwell in the North Pacific.

★ **Most albatrosses** are white or pale gray in color, with black wing tips. Some albatrosses have shades of brown.

★ **The wandering albatross** has the largest wingspan of all birds, at about 12 feet. It can grow up to 4.5 feet in length, with females being smaller than males.

★ **Albatrosses** have a sharp bill with a hooked upper jaw. They also have tubular nostrils and webbed feet. Their long, narrow wings make them powerful gliders.

★ **These birds** have an acute sense of smell that helps them find nest sites in the dark.

▶ *Albatrosses are also known as gooney birds. Once airborne, these graceful creatures can glide for hours without flapping their wings.*

⭐ **Albatrosses** prey on squid, cuttlefish, and small marine creatures. Unlike gulls, these large birds can drink seawater.

⭐ **Of all seabirds**, albatrosses spend the most time at sea. They even sleep while floating on the surface of the ocean. They come ashore only during the breeding season.

⭐ **Albatrosses nest** in colonies on remote islands. Most of them have complex mating dances and may even change color during courtship.

⭐ **These birds** can travel thousands of miles. Adult albatrosses often go out into the sea in search of food for their young. Since the distances are great, the parents swallow the prey and regurgitate the food into the chick's mouth when they arrive back at the nest.

⭐ **There is a superstition** among sailors that killing an albatross brings bad luck. This belief forms the theme of Samuel Taylor Coleridge's famous poem "The Rime of the Ancient Mariner."

Petrels

There are about 100 known species of petrels. Although storm petrels and diving petrels are different from true petrels, all are closely related.

Most petrels are migratory. A distinctive feature of this bird is the tubular nostrils on its bill. Storm petrels, however, have only one opening, serving both nostrils.

▼ Petrels are closely related to albatrosses and are also excellent fliers. These birds spend most of their lives at sea, coming ashore only to nest.

Fulmar

Wilson's storm petrel

Leach's storm petrel

- **Petrels**, like albatrosses, are found mainly in southern waters.

- **Most petrels** breed in colonies on islands in the Southern Hemisphere. Some gadfly petrels breed farther north on islands such as the Hawaiian Islands.

- **The petrel's bill** is hooked at the end. The bill consists of several plates, which fit into grooves.

DID YOU KNOW?

Petrels can flutter and hover over the water, stirring up small fish and plankton that they pick up with their bill. While doing this, it looks as if they are walking on the water.

- **Common varieties of petrels** include the gray petrel, the snow petrel, the Westland petrel, and the giant petrel. The giant petrel is the largest and can grow up to a length of 3 feet, which is bigger even than some albatrosses.

- **Storm petrels** are so named because they are often seen along the coast immediately before storms. This group includes the smallest species among seabirds. Some storm petrels are just 5 inches long, while the largest are only 10 inches long.

- **Diving petrels** can be distinguished from others in the group by their nostrils, which point upward instead of forward. Unlike other petrels, they do not migrate.

- **Petrels** do not usually dive very deep into the water. Diving petrels, however, are excellent divers.

Murres and kittiwakes

* **Murres look** like smaller versions of penguins. These birds migrate up to 3,700 miles every year, covering the first 600 miles by swimming.

* **These birds** have a thin, pointed bill and a small, rounded tail. Like all seabirds, they are good swimmers and can dive to depths of 65 feet in search of food.

* **Murres** spend most of the year at sea, in waters that offer plenty of prey. They nest in colonies on cliffs or on rocky terrain along the coast.

* **There are two species** of murres: the common murre and the thick-billed murre. Although both species look similar, the common murre's back is lighter in color during summer compared to that of the thick-billed murre. In winter, a white streak is visible behind the common murre's eye.

▼ Common murres come to land only to nest. They spend the rest of their time at sea.

▶ *Kittiwakes are the only species in the gull family that make nests on cliffs.*

★ **Thick-billed murres** breed in large colonies on cliff ledges in and around the Arctic and subarctic regions. They are 16–19 inches in length, while common murres are slightly smaller.

★ **Kittiwakes** belong to the gull family. They are found in shades of white, gray, and black. Their wings are mostly gray, with black tips. Juvenile kittiwakes have a distinctive black "W" band across the length of their wings.

★ **It is believed** that kittiwakes were named because of their call, which sounds like "kitti-wake!" They can also be called frost gulls or winter gulls.

★ **Unlike other gulls**, kittiwakes do not have a hind toe and do not scavenge or prey on other birds. They feed on fish and live more at sea than other gulls.

★ **Kittiwakes** are hardly seen on land except during the breeding season. They nest in large colonies on narrow cliff ledges.

★ **There are two species** of kittiwakes: the black-legged kittiwake and the red-legged kittiwake. The black-legged kittiwake is the most common.

Frigate birds and boobies

▲ *The male frigate bird inflates his scarlet throat pouch to attract a mate during breeding time.*

★ **Frigate birds** are related to pelicans and cormorants. All five species in this family are found along tropical coasts. They are named after the battleship frigate because they attack other seabirds and steal their prey.

★ **These water birds** are big, and their wings are large in proportion to the rest of their body. Frigates cannot walk or swim. They take off from cliffs or trees.

★ **Frigate birds** have long, pointed wings and forked tails, and they fly very fast.

★ **There are two well-known species** of frigate birds: the great frigate and the magnificent frigate bird. The great frigate bird is more widely distributed and can be found along the tropical coasts of the Pacific and Indian oceans.

★ **Male frigate birds** have a black, glossy body with a red patch of skin at the throat, called the gular sac. During the mating season, the male fills the sac with air, causing it to inflate like a balloon. It then waggles its head and shakes its wings to attract the females.

⭐ **Boobies** are close relatives of frigate birds. They are largely found in the tropical and subtropical coasts and islands.

⭐ **These water birds** are large, with webbed feet and long, pointed wings. These birds also have a long, sharp bill.

⭐ **Their webbed feet** help them to swim and dive. They are good divers and catch fish for food. Boobies nest in large colonies near the coast.

⭐ **The name "booby"** comes from the Spanish word *bobo*, which means "stupid." Sailors thought these birds were silly because they allowed themselves to be caught easily.

⭐ **Well-known booby species** include the blue-footed, red-footed, Peruvian, and brown boobies.

▼ *The blue-footed booby is commonly found in the Galápagos Islands.*

Terns

* **Terns are members** of the gull family. They are found in most seas and oceans of the world, but are more common in the tropical and subtropical regions.

* **There are about 50 species** of terns. Of these, the arctic, Caspian, royal, and common terns are well known.

* **Terns are lighter**, smaller, and more streamlined than gulls. They have a long, forked tail, and because of this they are often called sea swallows.

* **These birds** are usually found in shades of black, gray, and white. Some terns have black markings on their head. They have sharp, pointed bills.

* **Terns are faster** than gulls and can hover. They rarely go far without flapping their wings and usually do not alight on the water unless to catch prey.

★ **The smallest** tern is the least tern, which is only 8 inches long. It has a wingspan of about 20 inches. The Caspian tern is the largest tern. It can reach over 20 inches in length and has a wingspan of over 50 inches.

★ **Terns do not swim**. However, they are skilled at fishing and can dive into the water to catch their prey. Apart from fish, terns also eat other small marine creatures and insects.

★ **The male tern** often performs a complex fish flight to attract females. He carries a small fish in his beak and flies low over a female sitting on the ground.

★ **Royal terns** are seen in large, dense colonies on sandy beaches. Their nests, which they make on the ground, are often washed away, but they rebuild them.

▼ *Most terns nest in huge colonies on the beach. Some species also nest on trees, cliffs, and rocks.*

Arctic terns

✴ **Like all terns**, the arctic tern is a member of the gull family. This seabird is known for its long migratory trips.

✴ **The arctic tern** is found in the Arctic and subarctic regions of Asia, Europe, and North America.

▼ Arctic terns live for at least 30 years, during which time they fly more than 500,000 miles.

★ **In the fall**, these birds travel south all the way to the Antarctic region. This trip from the Arctic to the Antarctic and back measures over 25,000 miles.

★ **The distance** that arctic terns cover during migration is the longest for any bird. It takes the species more than eight months to complete this journey.

★ **After spending** the northern summer in the Arctic, the bird flies to Antarctica for the southern summer. Because of this, the arctic tern experiences more daylight than any other creature.

★ **Arctic terns** are not very large birds. However, some can grow to over 16 inches in length, from bill to tail.

★ **They are usually gray**, with a white underside and a black-topped head. The bill and feet are dark red. The webbed feet of arctic terns are fairly small, which means these birds cannot swim well.

★ **Arctic terns** stay away from the water as much as possible. They plunge into the water in search of small fish to eat, quickly swooping down to catch fish that are close to the surface of the water. Arctic terns also eat squid, krill, shrimps, and insects.

★ **Most arctic terns** nest in colonies on coasts and islands. They lay eggs on open ground, and like all terns they protect their young and nests.

★ **Arctic terns** are often confused with common terns. However, the bill of the arctic tern is much sharper, and its feet and legs are smaller.

Puffins

🌟 **Puffins** are closely related to murres. These waterbirds are found mainly around cold Arctic waters. Puffins have short, dumpy bodies, and are clumsy on land and in flight.

🌟 **There are four species** of puffins: the rhinoceros auklet, the Atlantic puffin, the horned puffin, and the tufted puffin.

🌟 **The Atlantic puffin** is the best known. Also called the common puffin, this species is found along the west coasts of Europe and off Maine in North America.

🌟 **Puffins are known** for their brightly colored bills, the shape of which resembles the beak of a parrot. The puffin, therefore, is also called the "sea parrot."

🌟 **The bill** may be bright red, orange, blue, or green. However, in winter it becomes dull gray in color.

🌟 **The tongue** and the upper part of the bill have spikes that help puffins hold onto several fish at a time.

🌟 **Puffins** have webbed feet that help them swim. They dive underwater to search for food. Each dive can last up to one minute.

🌟 **These birds** have thick, waterproof feathers to protect them from wet and cold climates. This, coupled with their ability to drink salt water, helps puffins live out at sea for months at a time.

🌟 **Puffins breed** in colonies and are known to pair for life. They dig burrows on cliffs and in the ground using their bills and feet. The female lays a single egg in the burrow.

▶ Puffins can store a number of fish in their bills to carry them back to their nests. On average, they can carry about ten fish at a time.

Penguins

★ **Penguins** are flightless seabirds. There are about 17 species of penguins, most of which live in the Antarctic region.

★ **Some species** are found as far north as the Galápagos Islands. Smaller penguin species are found in warmer waters.

▶ *A gentoo penguin and chicks. These social birds live in large groups called colonies.*

- **Larger penguins** are better at retaining heat, so they can live closer to the South Pole. The emperor penguin is the tallest at 4 feet, while the smallest is the fairy penguin, or the little blue penguin, which is less than 16 inches in height.

- **Penguins** have a thick layer of fat that protects them from the freezing temperatures of the region. Their coats are waterproof.

- **These flightless birds** have black heads and wings, and a white underside. They have sharp bills and a short tail.

- **Penguins** do not use their wings for flying. Instead, the wings act like flippers that help them swim. These birds are good divers and swimmers, and can move in water at great speeds in search of small fish and krill.

- **On land**, penguins waddle about clumsily. They are often seen sliding down slopes on their bellies.

- **Adélie penguins** are known to waddle over 200 miles every year to reach their breeding grounds. These birds depend on the sun to navigate across the ice. Once the sun sets, they are at risk of losing their way.

- **Rockhopper penguins** have a tuft of yellow feathers on their head. They are called rockhoppers because they jump around from rock to rock.

- **Penguins have been hunted** extensively by humans for their fat and skin. Their natural enemies are sharks, whales, and leopard seals.

Emperor penguins

* **Emperor penguins** are the tallest of all penguin species. They are also the heaviest seabirds. An adult emperor penguin weighs about 100 pounds.

* **These seabirds live** along the coasts of Antarctica and are well adapted to the freezing temperatures there.

* **In addition** to using their huge fat reserves, emperor penguins also huddle together in order to keep each other warm. They take turns moving to the center of the group to warm up.

* **Their heads** and wings are black in color, while the abdomen is white and the back is bluish-gray. Emperor penguins also have bright orange or golden patches near their ears.

* **Emperor penguins** dive to great depths in search of food, which they catch in their sharp beaks. They can dive to depths of more than 800 feet and hold their breath underwater for almost 15 minutes.

* **Their diet** consists of fish, squid, and crustaceans.

* **These are the only** penguins to breed in the harsh winter of the Antarctic. The male penguins have a warm layer of skin between their legs and lower abdomen called the "brood pouch."

* **Emperor penguins** do not build nests. After courtship, the female lays a single egg and leaves it in the care of the male. She then goes to sea to hunt for food. Meanwhile, the male holds the egg on his feet and covers it with his brood pouch.

⭐ **The egg** takes about 60 days to hatch. During this time, the male emperor penguin braves icy winds and fierce storms to protect the egg on his feet. He even starves himself through this period.

⭐ **After about two months** of hunting at sea, the female returns with food. She regurgitates the food to feed the newborn chick. The male goes out to sea, leaving the female to care for the chick.

▼ Emperor penguins get their dark coloring as they mature. Chicks are gray in color.

Whales

⭐ **Whales are the largest** and heaviest animals on the planet. Their size can range from 6 feet to more than 100 feet.

⭐ **Being mammals**, whales breathe with their lungs. They do not have gills. The nostrils of whales, called blowholes, are located on top of the head.

Gray whale

Minke whale

Bowhead whale

Blue whale

Fin whale

▲ *Baleen whales are also known as great whales. This group includes gray, minke, bowhead, fin, and the mighty blue whale.*

- **When underwater**, whales need to hold their breath. They come up to the surface and open their blowholes to breathe. After taking in the required amount of air, these animals dive into the water again. The blowholes remain closed underwater.

- **The spout, or blow**, that can be seen rising from the blowhole is not water. It is actually stale air that condenses and vaporizes the moment it is released into the atmosphere. This spout can sometimes reach a height of 30 feet.

DID YOU KNOW?

Whales use a series of moans and clicks to communicate amongst themselves. Most of these are either too low or too high for humans to hear. Blue and fin whales are believed to produce the loudest sounds of any animal.

- **Whales are divided** into two main groups: toothed whales and baleen whales. Together, these groups consist of 81 known species.

- **Toothed whales** have small teeth in their jaws, which are used to kill prey like fish and squid. This group includes dolphins, killer whales, sperm whales, beluga whales, and porpoises.

- **Toothed whales** emit sound waves that are bounced off an object, revealing its size, shape, and location. This is known as echolocation. Toothed whales can even use this technique to distinguish between prey and non-prey objects.

- **Baleen whales**, on the other hand, are toothless. They trap their prey in sievelike structures that hang from their upper jaws.

Dolphins

* **Dolphins** are close relatives of whales and form a large part of the toothed whales group. They have a beak-shaped snout and are extremely active and playful.

* **Powerful swimmers**, dolphins are found in all oceans. The shape of their body and their big flippers help in rapid movement. Dolphins are often spotted riding on waves, probably to conserve energy.

* **Dolphins** are good at diving deep into the ocean and also leaping into the air. Many of them can leap as high as 20 feet. They can even turn somersaults before landing in the water with a splash.

* **Like baleen whales**, dolphins have blowholes on top of their head. They surface every two minutes to breathe, before diving under again.

* **Dolphins use** echolocation to hunt and navigate through cloudy waters. They emit a series of high-pitched sound pulses, which bounce off prey or obstacles, enabling dolphins to locate them.

* **These animals** hunt in groups. They chase their prey, surround it, and catch it with their powerful jaws. Dolphins have numerous conical teeth.

DID YOU KNOW?
Some scientists believe that dolphins have a language of their own, heard by humans in the form of whistling sounds. Some even believe that they are able to understand sign language.

▲ Bottlenose dolphins usually swim at speeds of 3–7 mph, but sometimes they can exceed 20 mph.

The smallest dolphin is the tucuxi dolphin, which is just 3 feet long. Bottlenose dolphins can reach a length of over 11 feet, while common dolphins are about 8 feet long.

The killer whale is the largest member of the dolphin family. It can reach a length of almost 30 feet. Like others in the family, the killer whale is very intelligent and can be trained to do tricks.

The playful nature of dolphins has made them extremely popular, especially with children. They are common sights in aquariums.

Dolphins used to be hunted for their meat and oil. Until recently, thousands used to die every year by getting caught in fishing nets.

Porpoises

⭐ **Porpoises are small**, toothed whales. They are close relatives of dolphins, and are often mistaken for them.

⭐ **They are usually smaller than dolphins**, and not as sleek and streamlined. Porpoises rarely grow to more than 7 feet. They are usually gray, blue, or black in color.

▼ Porpoises are smaller cousins of whales and dolphins. Most species of porpoises live in small groups of up to five.

Spectacled porpoise

Burmeister's porpoise

Common porpoise

⚓ **The dorsal fin** of a porpoise is triangular, whereas the dolphin's is curved. Porpoises do not have a beak.

⚓ **There are several varieties** of porpoises, including Dall's and the spectacled porpoise. The harbor porpoise, also called the common porpoise, is the best known.

⚓ **Harbor porpoises** are found in cold, northern waters and are known to frequent bays and estuaries. They have a small body and dorsal fin.

⚓ **There are two varieties** of Dall's porpoises—the dalli type and the truei type. Both are found in the northern Pacific Ocean.

⚓ **Dall's porpoises** are known for the splash they make in the water with their tails. This is referred to as the "rooster-tail splash," and has earned this species the nickname of "spray porpoise."

⚓ **Another well-known species** is the spectacled porpoise, found in the South Atlantic. The upper part of its body is bluish-black, while the lower half is white.

⚓ **Spectacled porpoises** have black patches around their eyes, which are surrounded by a white line. These resemble spectacles.

⚓ **Other varieties of porpoises** include the Burmeister's porpoise, commonly found off the coasts of South America. It is named after the German biologist Hermann Burmeister, who gave this species the scientific name *spinipinnis*, meaning "spiny fin." This was due to the blunt, thornlike structures, called tubercles, along the edges of the porpoise's fins.

Whale facts

★ **Baleen whales** have a huge mouth that contains rows of baleen plates. These plates have fringed edges, like a comb, that filter plankton from the water.

★ **Whales of this group** swim with their mouths open and take in huge quantities of water containing krill and other small marine creatures. These creatures get trapped in the fringed edges of the baleen. The whale licks the food off the baleen and swallows it.

★ **Baleen**, also called whalebone, was once valued for its plasticlike attributes. Great whales were widely hunted for their baleen. However, with the wide availability of good-quality plastic, the demand for baleen has diminished.

★ **Heat loss is greater** in water than it is on land at the same temperature. Whales have a thick layer of fat, called blubber, between the skin and the flesh that preserves body heat.

★ **Blubber also helps** to keep the animals afloat and is a source of stored energy. Until recently, it was extensively used in the manufacture of cosmetics and ointments.

★ **Toothed whales** have smaller mouths than great whales. However, unlike meat-eating animals of the land, the teeth of these whales are uniform in size and shape.

★ **Most whales swim** and feed in groups called pods. Many whales are known to migrate long distances between their feeding places and breeding grounds.

★ **Whales** sometimes pop their head above the surface and float motionless. This is known as "logging."

🌟 **Certain whales**, like humpback whales, are very acrobatic and can leap out of the water. This is known as "breaching." They also indulge in "lob-tailing"—sticking out their tail and then splashing it in the water.

🌟 **Some whales** also lift their head vertically out of the water before slipping back below. This is known as "spyhopping." It is believed that they do this to obtain a view above the surface.

▲ *Humpbacks rise through shoals of fish with their mouths open. They scoop up water, push it out through the baleen, and swallow the food left inside their mouths.*

Blue whale

★ **Blue whales** are the largest creatures to have ever lived on this planet. They are even larger than the mighty dinosaurs that lived millions of years ago.

★ **Their average length** is 80 feet, but some can grow to more than 100 feet. Brachiosaurus, the largest dinosaur, was only 70 feet in length.

★ **These whales** are blue-gray in color, with light patches on their backs. Sometimes, the underside of this animal can be yellowish in color. This is caused by a kind of algae.

▼ *The blue whale is far bigger than any other creature on the planet. It can make a grunting sound that is louder than a space rocket taking off!*

🌟 **The body** is streamlined, with a large tail fin. The dorsal fin is small, while the tail is thick and large. Blue whales have splashguards in front of their two blowholes. The spout of a blue whale is vertical and can be 30–40 feet high.

🌟 **Blue whales** are migratory animals. They live near the tropics during winter and migrate toward icy waters in summer.

🌟 **The diet** of a blue whale consists of small fish, plankton, and krill in enormous quantities. They can eat over 4 tons of krill every day.

🌟 **These whales** have been known to gather in groups of 60 or more. However, they are largely solitary animals.

🌟 **Blue whales** are relatively slow swimmers. However, when threatened, these animals can swim at a speed of over 20 mph.

🌟 **Merciless hunting** over several decades has caused the blue whale population to decline drastically. It is currently an endangered species, and only 5,000 are thought to exist worldwide.

Right whale

⭐ **Right whales** got their name from the fact that whalers thought that they were the "right" whales to hunt, since they were easy to approach, floated when they died, and provided large quantities of oil and whalebone.

⭐ **These great whales** have a large head and a bow-shaped lower jaw. They are easily recognized because of the presence of light-colored wartlike growths called callosities. These are usually located on the head, near the blowhole and around the eyes and jaws.

⭐ **The average length** of right whales is 50–60 feet. They are dark gray, black, or light brown in color, with white patches on the underside.

⭐ **These whales** can be found in cool, temperate waters in both hemispheres. They migrate to warmer waters when they breed.

▼ *The bowhead whale's baleen hangs like a huge curtain, big enough for ten people to hide behind.*

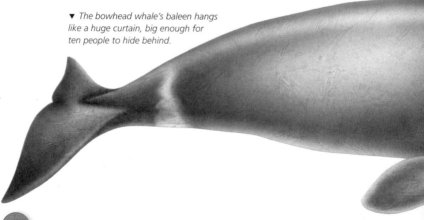

★ **Based on certain minor differences**, especially in the shape of their skulls and habitat, right whales are broadly divided into two species. Northern right whales are found in the Northern Hemisphere, while southern right whales live in southern waters.

★ **There are two other species** in the right whale family. They are the bowhead whale and the pygmy right whale.

★ **Bowhead whales** live in cold waters in the north. Like all arctic whales, they do not have a dorsal fin.

★ **Pygmy right whales** are rare and are found mostly in temperate waters in the Southern Hemisphere. They are small and are not known to grow more than 16 feet in length.

★ **These great whales** prefer to live close to the surface and are filter feeders. They swim just below the water's surface and feed on krill, shrimps, and small fish.

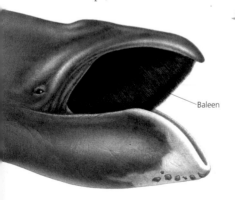

Baleen

★ **Right whales**, despite their size, are very acrobatic. They often flap their fins on the surface, and can be seen breaching. But they particularly love to "sail," when they stand on their heads and wave their tail flukes in the air for up to two minutes.

Gray whale

★ **Gray whales** are gray in color, with mottled patterns in lighter shades. They have a low hump instead of a dorsal fin and their heads are covered with parasites, such as barnacles and whale lice.

★ **These whales** can grow up to 50 feet long. They have a layer of blubber that is nearly 10 inches thick. Their head is slightly arched and pointed.

★ **They are commonly** found along the coastal regions of the North Pacific Ocean. In winter, they breed in the shallow waters off the coast of Mexico, and in summer they make their way back to the Bering Sea in the north.

★ **Every year during autumn**, gray whales embark on a migration of almost 12,000 miles. This is believed to be the longest migration of any mammal.

▼ *A young whale is called a calf. Newborn gray whales are up to 16 feet in length and weigh more than half a ton.*

 Gray whales travel south to Mexico in winter to have their calves.

 In summer the whales swim back to the food-rich waters off the coast of Alaska.

▶ *The California gray whale spends almost one-third of its life migrating, from the Chuchki Sea in the Arctic Ocean to the Baja Peninsula off the coast of Mexico and back.*

✳ **Gray whales** are bottom feeders. Their diet consists of shrimps, krill, and marine worms. On average, gray whales eat more than 2,000 pounds of food per day. These whales turn on their sides to scrape up the mud on the ocean floor, leaving huge holes in the seabed. They use their baleen to filter the creatures in the silt.

✳ **Gray whales** are one of the most active great whales. They often indulge in lobtailing (waving the tail fin in the air) and spyhopping (sticking their heads above the surface and turning around gently).

✳ **Until the 1700s**, there were three populations of gray whales in the world. Of these, the North Atlantic species has been hunted to extinction.

✳ **Today**, there are about 24,000 gray whales in the world. This is believed to be the same number that existed before extensive hunting of these whales began in the 18th century.

Humpback whale

* **Humpback whales** are large baleen whales. They are found in most parts of the world. During summer they migrate to the icy waters in the north and south. In winter, they breed in warm, tropical waters.

* **They have a round**, flat head that has fleshy bumps called tubercles. The body is black or gray, with mottled white patches. The underside is off-white.

* **Humpbacks** can grow up to 50 feet in length. At almost 16 feet, its flippers are the longest among whales. Humpback whales are named after a hump on which the whale's dorsal fin is located. This is most pronounced when the whale dives.

* **The tail fin** measures nearly 18 feet across and has black and white patterns. Since no two humpback whales have the same pattern on their tails, scientists use it to identify and monitor them.

* **Male humpbacks** are known for their unusual and eerie songs. The sounds vary from high-pitched squeaks to deep wails and are usually heard during the breeding season.

* **They feed** on shrimps, krill, and small fish. Humpbacks have various methods of feeding. These include lunge-feeding, tail-flicking, and bubble-netting.

* **In lunge-feeding**, the humpback opens its mouth wide and swims through a group of prey, often surfacing with food in its mouth.

* **When tail-flicking**, the whale lies with its belly below the surface. It uses its tail to flick the prey into the air and into its mouth.

✳ **Bubble-netting** is the most spectacular of all feeding habits and the most commonly used by the humpback. The whale slaps its flippers around a school of fish, creating a wall of bubbles. This action forces the fish to move to the surface in large groups, making them easy prey.

▲ Humpbacks have lots of lumps and bumps on their heads called tubercles. Hard-shelled sea creatures called barnacles also live there.

Sperm whale

★ **The largest** of the toothed whales are sperm whales. Males can grow up to 65 feet long and weigh 50 tons. The whale in Herman Melville's novel *Moby-Dick* was a sperm whale.

★ **Sperm whales** are named for the highly valued spermaceti oil, which is a waxy substance found in the sperm whale's head. This substance is believed to help the whale during deep dives.

★ **Spermaceti oil** is used by Arctic natives as an ointment. It is also used to make high-quality candles that burn with a clear flame.

★ **Sperm whales** have an extremely large head, which is square and blunt. The head is almost one-third of its total body length. These whales have the largest brain in the animal kingdom.

DID YOU KNOW?
Sperm whales produce a waxlike substance known as ambergris. This is used in perfumes to make their scent last longer.

⭐ **Sperm whales** are dark brown or dark gray in color and their skin is wrinkled. They have broad, powerful tail flukes, but their flippers are short and stubby.

⭐ **These whales** have only one blowhole and the spout is angled. Large conical teeth are located on the lower jaw and fit into sockets on the upper jaw.

⭐ **Sperm whales** are good swimmers. Capable of diving to depths of 10,000 feet, these whales are the deepest divers among sea mammals. After a long dive, sperm whales need to stay on the surface for 15 minutes to replenish oxygen.

⭐ **Sometimes** sperm whales can be spotted floating on the water with a part of their head popping out above the surface.

⭐ **Sperm whales** can hold their breath for more than one hour as they dive down and down. They use clicks of sound, which they hear bouncing back off nearby objects, to find their prey in the darkness.

⭐ **Many sperm whales** bear injuries from the suckers of giant squid. Scientists have mounted cameras on sperm whales in order to capture giant squid on video.

◄ Sperm whales have been known to dive to depths of up to 10,000 feet in search of their favorite food, the giant squid.

245

Killer whale

⭐ **Killer whales**, also known as orcas, are the largest dolphins. Despite their name, killer whales have more in common with dolphins than with great whales. Hence they are considered a part of the dolphin family.

⭐ **They have a black body** with white patches on their underside and behind each eye.

⭐ **These animals** are found in oceans across the world, but prefer to live in colder temperate waters. They do not migrate in summer like great whales but can swim for long distances.

★ **Killer whales** prefer to live close to the coast. Their average length is 26–30 feet. They have sharp, hooked teeth, which they use to rip their prey apart.

★ *Dephinus orca* was the earliest scientific name for the killer whale. It meant "demon dolphin."

★ **It is believed** that the name "killer whale" might itself have been derived from the name "whale killer." This name was given to these animals by 18th-century whalers who saw them feeding on other whales and dolphins.

★ **The diet of orcas** is varied. However, they largely prey on fish, squid, sharks, and warm-blooded animals such as seals, seabirds, and larger whales, including blue whales.

★ **Orcas are known** as the "wolves of the sea." Like wolves, they hunt in groups and hence are able to tackle prey of all shapes and sizes.

★ **The pods of killer whales** are divided into resident and transient pods. Resident pods can consist of 5–50 members who communicate frequently using whistles and high-pitched screams.

★ **Transient pods** are smaller, with a maximum of seven members who feed mainly on marine mammals. Members of transient pods do not communicate frequently with each other.

◀ *A killer whale suddenly appears out of the surf and tries to grab an unsuspecting sea lion before it has time to escape.*

Pilot whale

★ **Pilot whales** belong to a group of dolphins called blackfish. Orcas also belong to this group.

★ **These animals** have a small beak and a rounded head. They are dark brown or gray in color and have a distinct, swept-back dorsal fin.

▼ Pilot whales are toothed whales. They are active hunters and feed on squid and fish.

- **Pilot whales** have slight patches behind their eyes and dorsal fins. They are smaller than orcas and can grow as long as 23 feet. They largely feed on octopus and squid.

- **There are two** species of pilot whales—the short-finned and the long-finned. Apart from their habitats, most of the characteristics of these species are similar.

- **The short-finned variety** can be found in warm tropical waters and cooler subtropical waters. They cannot adapt well to shallow waters.

- **Long-finned pilot whales** live in cold waters in the north, near Greenland and Norway, and in the South Atlantic Ocean.

- **Pilot whales** are known for their strong family units. They live in close-knit pods of six or more. Females never leave the pod they were born in.

- **Members of a pod** are known to stick together, even in times of danger. It is believed that when the leader of the pod becomes disoriented due to illness or loses its way in shallow water, it gets stranded. In such situations, the rest of the pod follows suit. This phenomenon is common in the long-finned variety.

- **Female pilot whales** feed their young for several years. They will also take care of the young of their sisters and daughters.

- **This whale**, particularly the long-finned variety, was extensively hunted for its meat. Whalers in Newfoundland and the Faroe Islands used to drive large groups of pilot whales ashore and kill them.

Narwhal

🌟 **Narwhals**, like belugas, belong to the dolphin family. Both these species are white whales. The long tusk on their snout is a distinctive feature.

🌟 **The word** *narwhal* means "corpse whale" in an ancient Scandinavian language. Its mottled white color makes it look like a corpse floating on the water.

🌟 **Narwhals** can be found in northern Arctic seas. These rarely sighted whales can survive in the coldest temperatures.

▼ *Adult male narwhals often carry scars of brutal tusk fights on their head.*

★ **These whales** have a small, round head, and a small beak. Their skin has white patches and a dark stripe. Like belugas, narwhals lack a dorsal fin.

★ **Narwhals** have a thick layer of blubber, which accounts for over one-third of their body weight.

★ **These whales** can grow up to 16 feet, without the tusk. The tusk can grow to more than 10 feet in length.

★ **This toothed whale** has only two teeth, both in the upper jaw. The left tooth grows into the whale's unusual tusk. Sometimes both teeth grow to form double tusks. In this case, the right tusk is smaller than the left one.

★ **These tusks** are seen only in males. However, females with smaller tusks have been seen. The tusk has earned the narwhal the nickname "unicorn of the sea."

★ **Some scientists** believe that the whales use their tusks to fence with rival males during the mating season. Other scientists believe that narwhals also use their tusks to spear prey and poke holes in the ice.

★ **The narwhal's tusk** is thought to possess medicinal properties. It is also used to make fine jewelry. For years, this whale has been hunted for its tusk as well as its skin and oil.

Beluga

* **Beluga whales** are fascinating creatures. Their playful nature, along with their unusual color, makes them popular attractions in aquariums.

* **Related to dolphins**, the adult beluga whale is milky white in color. Its name is derived from the Russian word *belukha*, meaning "white." Belugas have a thick, stout body; a small beak; and a prominent forehead, which is called a "melon."

* **The color** of the whale matches its surroundings. This whale lives close to icebergs in the Arctic Ocean. Young belugas, however, are gray in color.

* **Belugas** do not have a dorsal fin, which makes swimming under ice much easier.

* **Compared with other whales**, belugas have narrower necks. Unlike most other baleen and toothed whales, belugas can also nod and shake their heads from side to side.

* ***Delphinapterus leucas***, the scientific name of the beluga, means "white dolphin without wings," referring to the absence of a dorsal fin in this species.

* **The beluga's diet** consists of crab, squid, shrimp, and fish. They love salmon and often swim into the mouths of rivers to feed on them. They use their teeth to grab prey rather than to chew.

★ **Belugas** are very social and tend to travel in groups consisting of 5–20 members. These groups are usually led by a single male. During migrations, the groups can exceed 10,000 members.

★ **These whales** emit various sounds, from whistles to chirps and squeaks. They are the most vocal whales, earning them the nickname of "sea canaries."

★ **Belugas are hunted** by killer whales. The young are often killed by polar bears. It is not uncommon to find adult belugas bearing scars from polar bear attacks.

▼ *The young beluga is born dark gray or pinkish-gray. It gradually becomes lighter, but it may not take on its all-white coloration until it is more than five years old.*

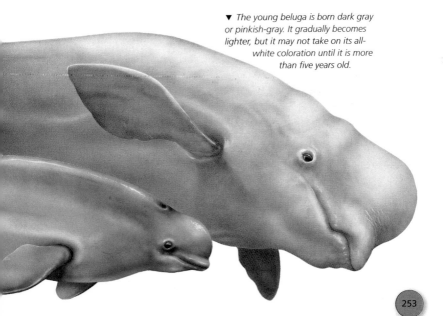

Seals

★ **Seals are marine mammals** that belong to the same group as walruses and sea lions. Together, these animals are called pinnipeds, which means "fin-footed." All of them have limbs that look like fins.

★ **There are two families of seals:** true seals and eared seals. Unlike eared seals, true seals do not have external ear flaps.

★ **There are 19 species of true seals**, making them the largest group of pinnipeds. Eared seals consist of sea lions and fur seals.

▼ Most seals live in cold regions. They have a thick coat of fur that keeps them warm. These animals also have a layer of fat, called blubber, under their skin, which not only provides warmth but also serves as a source of energy when food is scarce.

- **The limbs of seals** are modified into powerful flippers that help in swimming. Their strong, torpedo-shaped body, coupled with the ability to store oxygen, make them great swimmers.

- **Eared seals** have long rear flippers that are more mobile than those of true seals. Their front flippers are also large and more powerful. Eared seals mainly use their front flippers to paddle through water.

- **Seals** spend most of their lives in water, but they have to come ashore to breed and nurse their young. Some live at sea for several months at a time, while others return to the shore every day.

- **Seals are clumsy on land**. They slide along the shore with difficulty. However, the large flippers of eared seals are better adapted for moving on land.

- **Seals range in size** from 3–13 feet. Galápagos fur seals and ringed seals are the smallest species. The largest is the male southern elephant seal, which can grow to 16 feet in length.

- **The diet** of seals consists mainly of fish, squid, crabs, and shellfish. Leopard seals are among the most aggressive hunters. They kill other seals and penguins for food. They are also known to have injured divers.

- **Killer whales**, sharks, and polar bears are the natural predators of seals. They are endangered because of excessive hunting by humans for their meat, fat, and fur. The Caribbean monk seal is now extinct due to excessive hunting.

Harp seal

Harp seals are found in the cold waters of the Arctic and the North Atlantic oceans. They get their name from the harp-shaped mark on their back.

These seals have a silvery-gray coat of fur and catlike whiskers. The harp-shaped mark on the back is dark brown or black in color, and is less distinct in females.

Newborn seals have a white coat, hence their common name, whitecoats. Since the color of their coat matches their surroundings, predators find it hard to spot young harp seals.

The pups are born with yellowish fur, which turns white after a couple of days. This white fur starts to molt in two-week-old pups to give way to a silvery-gray coat with irregular dark spots.

Adult males grow up to 5.5 feet in length and weigh about 280 pounds. Female harp seals are smaller in size. Pups are usually about 20 pounds at birth.

These seals are good swimmers, and are known to dive to great depths in search of food. They can also stay underwater for over 15 minutes at a stretch.

Harp seals are highly social, migratory creatures. Long before the approach of winter, they gather in huge numbers and head south toward their winter breeding grounds.

During the breeding season, thousands of harp seals gather on pack ice in dense breeding patches. Pups are born between February and March and are nursed for about two weeks.

* **Polar bears** are the main enemies of harp seals. Other predators include arctic foxes, killer whales, Greenland sharks, and walruses.

* **Harp seals** have been widely hunted for their meat and their coats. The pups were once killed for their white fur. Today, there are laws controlling harp seal hunting.

▼ *About five weeks after their birth, harp seal pups are left to fend for themselves. During this period the pups lose about 20 pounds of their body weight. This is because they are unable to hunt on their own for at least four weeks.*

257

Weddell seal

⭐ **Weddell seals** are large, nonmigratory creatures commonly found in the southern Atlantic Ocean and around Antarctica.

⭐ **These large seals are named** after the British explorer James Weddell, who first described them.

▲ *The coats of adult Weddell seals are normally spotted and bluish-gray in color. The pups have a lighter, grayish-brown coat.*

- **Weddell seals** can measure over 10 feet in length. The females are usually bigger than the males.

- **These seals** have strong, modified front teeth that point forward. They can use them to dig holes in the ice so that they can breathe while swimming in ice-covered water.

> **DID YOU KNOW?**
> Weddell seals are good swimmers and excellent divers. They are known to be the best divers of all seals, and can remain at depths of over 1,500 feet for more than an hour.

- **Weddell seals** blow air into cracks in the ice in order to draw out small prey.

- **The diet** of the Weddell seal consists mainly of fish such as cod and Antarctic silverfish. They also feed on crab, squid, and octopus.

- **Leopard seals** and killer whales are the main predators of the Weddell seal. These animals usually prey on the pups.

- **Weddell seals are** very noisy, especially underwater. They use a variety of calls to communicate among themselves. These sounds can also be heard from the surface of the water.

- **During the freezing winter**, these seals prefer to stay underwater rather than on land, since the water under the ice is warmer.

- **Weddell seals** have very good underwater vision. This helps them hunt for prey.

Monk seal

★ **Monk seals** are true seals, which means they do not have ear flaps. There are three kinds of monk seals: Mediterranean, Hawaiian, and Caribbean.

★ **It is believed that monk seals** got their name because their smooth brown coats resemble the robes of a Franciscan monk. They might have also been given this name because they lead a solitary life, much like monks do.

DID YOU KNOW?

History tells us that Christopher Columbus ordered his ship's crew to kill several Caribbean monk seals for food during an expedition. This marked the beginning of a cruel exploitation that eventually led to their extinction.

★ **Monk seals** are often referred to as "living fossils" because, according to fossil records, they have existed for about 15 million years.

★ **Mediterranean monk seals** are the most endangered of all seals. It is illegal to kill these seals, but they are still killed by fishermen who view them as pests that damage nets and eat fish stocks.

★ **Hawaiian monk seals** are the second most endangered seal species. They are found off the northwest coasts of the Hawaiian Islands.

★ **Hawaiian monk seals** were once killed in great numbers by seal hunters, or sealers, for their meat. Shark attacks are also responsible for the decline in their population.

★ **Male Hawaiian monk seals** are known to be very aggressive and often injure and kill the females and younger seals. This is known as "mobbing."

★ **Today**, there are only about 1,500 Hawaiian monk seals and 500 Mediterranean monk seals left in the world.

★ **The Caribbean monk seal**, also known as the West Indian monk seal, is extinct.

★ **This seal** was wiped out as a result of being extensively hunted by humans for its meat and fat. It was last sighted in 1952, off Seranilla Bank between Jamaica and Honduras.

▼ *Monk seals can dive to depths of about 1,500 feet in search of food. They can stay underwater for 15 minutes while hunting.*

Arctic seals

⭐ **Arctic seals** include harp seals, ringed seals, hooded seals, bearded seals, spotted seals, and ribbon seals.

⭐ **Ribbon seals** are named for the light-colored ribbon stripes around the head, front flippers, and posterior. These ribbon stripes start to appear at the age of four. They are more distinct in males than in females.

▼ Arctic seals bang their heads against ice on the water's surface to create breathing holes.

These seals have internal air sacs above their ribs. However, the use of these air sacs remains a mystery. Ribbon seals are the only species to have such air sacs.

Most arctic seals pull their front flippers together while moving on ice. Ribbon seals, however, move one flipper at a time.

Hooded seals are named for the inflatable "hood" on the top of their head. These hoods are found only in males, who also have inflatable nasal sacs. The male hooded seals inflate these sacs through one or both nostrils during courtship.

Bearded seals get their name from their prominent white whiskers, which they use to find food at the bottom of the ocean.

Ringed seals are the smallest of all pinnipeds and do not grow longer than 5 feet. They are named for the ring-shaped marks on their body. These are the most abundant arctic seals.

Spotted seals were once thought to be the same as harbor seals. Both these seals were referred to as "common seals."

Later it was realized that these seals were different. Harbor seals are found only in ice-free water, while spotted seals inhabit pack ice. Moreover, spotted seals are the only seals that breed in China.

Northern fur seal

✦ **Northern fur seals** are found in the cold waters of the North Pacific, particularly in the Bering Sea and the Okhotsk Sea.

✦ **These are** the only fur seals that are not found in the Southern Hemisphere.

✦ **Northern fur seals** are eared seals and have small external ears.

✦ **Like all other eared seals**, northern fur seals have modified flippers that help them to "walk" on land as well as swim.

✦ **A thick layer of fat**, or blubber, protects the northern fur seal from the extremely cold temperatures.

✦ **Adult males** are over 6.5 feet in length. The females are smaller at around 4.5 feet.

✦ **Northern fur seals** have dense fur, arranged in two layers. The coat has a thick undercoat of soft fur, covered by longer, coarser hair. These seals keep themselves warm by trapping air in their fur.

✦ **The diet** of northern fur seals includes a variety of fish, but they feed mainly on squid and octopus. They also eat herring, mackerel, and anchovies.

🌟 **Killer whales**, sharks, Steller's sea lions, and foxes are the main predators of northern fur seals.

🌟 **Northern fur seals** are also hunted for their meat and fur. A number of these seals have died by accidentally getting caught in fishing nets.

▼ *Male and female seals differ in color. The males have reddish-brown coats, while the females' coats are brownish-gray.*

Sea lions

★ **Sea lions** are eared seals. Unlike true seals, they have external ear flaps and their flippers are quite big.

★ **These extremely vocal animals** make a roaring noise, which gives them their name. They are brownish in color, with the males being darker than the females.

★ **Sea lions** use their flippers to swim and paddle in water as well as to walk on land. They can use their flippers as legs.

★ **Being highly social creatures**, sea lions swim in large groups.

★ **The Steller's sea lion** is the largest type of sea lion. The males can grow up to 10 feet in length. They are found in the northern waters of the Pacific Ocean, and are very common off Alaska.

★ **The diet** of a sea lion includes mainly fish, crab, squid, octopus, and clams. Steller's sea lions also feed on seals and small otters.

★ **The Steller's sea lion** and California sea lion are the best-known species. The former are tamed very easily and are popular attractions in aquariums.

★ **California sea lions** are found along the rocky western coast of North America. They are also found on the Galápagos Islands. The males are over 6.5 feet in length and the females are smaller.

★ **Killer whales** are the biggest enemies of sea lions. Sharks are also known to hunt California sea lions.

★ **A large number** of sea lions die as a result of getting caught in fishing nets. There are now laws restricting the hunting of sea lions. The Steller's sea lion has been declared as endangered.

▲ Sea lions nurse their pups for about one year. Duing this period, they leave
their pups to go hunting in the sea and return after five days to continue nursing.

Walruses

★ **Walruses are close relatives** of seals and sea lions. They are, however, much bigger and they also have tusks.

★ **These animals** are found in the Arctic region, at the edge of the polar ice sheet. There are two types of walruses: the Pacific and the Atlantic.

★ **Pacific walruses** live in and around the Bering Sea and off Siberia, Alaska, and Kamchatka in Russia. They are bigger than Atlantic walruses, which are found in the Canadian Arctic, the west Russian Arctic, and off the coast of Greenland.

DID YOU KNOW?
Walruses are noisy, social creatures. They often gather in huge numbers and bellow together.

⭐ **Walruses** are bulky creatures and can measure over 13 feet in length. The males are bigger than the females and their tusks are longer.

⭐ **The body** of the walrus is reddish-brown and has very little hair. Although it has a huge body, the head of the walrus is quite small in proportion.

⭐ **The tusks** are in fact a pair of elongated upper canine teeth. The walrus uses its tusks to defend itself and also as hooks for pulling itself out of the water onto the slippery ice.

⭐ **Like most marine mammals**, walruses have a thick layer of blubber that protects them from the cold.

⭐ **Walruses have four limbs** that are well adapted for walking on land.

⭐ **Polar bears** are the natural predators of the walrus on land. In water, killer whales are their biggest enemies. Walruses eat clams and mussels.

⭐ **People have killed walruses** in large numbers for their tusks. Inuits used to hunt them for their fat and meat.

◄ *Male walruses use their tusks to threaten rivals and thus establish dominance.*

269

Sea cows

⁕ **Manatees and dugongs** are both types of sea cows. They are large, thick-bodied mammals. Apart from whales and dolphins, sea cows are the only other mammals that live completely in water.

⁕ **Dugongs** are found in the tropical waters of the Indian and Pacific oceans, while manatees are found off the Caribbean Islands, the southeast United States, and West Africa.

⁕ **Sea cows** graze on sea grasses and other aquatic plants, hence their name. There are only four living species in this group, of which three belong to the manatee family.

⁕ **Sea cows** are also called sirenians, after the Sirens, or mermaids, of Greek mythology. It is believed that sailors probably mistook sea cows for creatures that were half human and half fish, thus giving rise to the mermaid legends.

⁕ **One of the largest species**, the Steller's sea cow, is now extinct. It was killed for its meat and skin. Since this slow-moving mammal could not defend itself, the population was completely wiped out.

⁕ **The Steller's sea cow** was first discovered in the Arctic waters in 1741 by the crew of the famous Russian explorer, Captain Vitus Bering.

⁕ **Manatees have a long**, rounded body that tapers toward the tail. Their average length is 11 feet. They have a short, square snout and are mostly gray in color.

⭐ **Dugongs and manatees** are related to elephants. Dugongs are very similar to manatees in both looks and habits, although some are slightly smaller.

⭐ **Both manatees and dugongs** are slow swimmers and use their forelimbs and tails to move in the water. They do not have hind limbs.

⭐ **Unlike the dugong,** the manatee's forelimbs are set very close to its head. The tail of the dugong is forked and pointed, while the manatee has a round, flat, paddlelike tail.

▶ *Manatees and dugongs are mammals and so they breathe air. They usually swim to the water's surface every few minutes.*

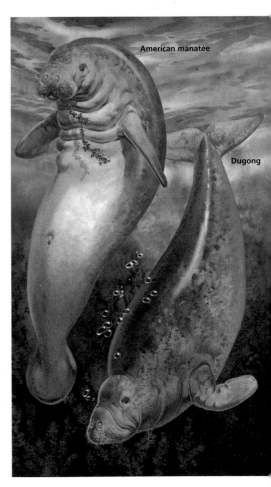

American manatee

Dugong

271

Sea otters

★ **Sea otters** are close relatives of weasels, skunks, ferrets, badgers, and minks.

★ **They are commonly** found along the coasts of the Pacific Ocean. Southern otters are found off California, northern otters near Alaska, and the Asian ones off Japan and Kamchatka, Russia.

▲ *Anchored to the kelp, a sea otter is free to crack open a crab shell—and snack!*

DID YOU KNOW?

The sea otter is the only marine mammal that does not have a layer of blubber to protect it from cold water. Instead, its dense fur traps warm air, keeping the animal warm.

- **Sea otters** live in waters close to the shore. They prefer rocky bottoms and coasts. Some, however, are found along sandy shores.

- **Sea otters are**, on average, around 5 feet long. These animals have an elongated, streamlined body and sharp claws on their feet.

- **The hind feet** are webbed, making sea otters fast swimmers. However, they move slowly on land. Sea otters spend most of their time in the water.

- **A dense coat** of fur protects sea otters from the cold waters of the Pacific Ocean. The coat is dark brown in color, and much paler at the head.

- **Sea otters** spend a lot of time grooming and cleaning their fur, which they comb with their claws.

- **The animals feed** on fish, crab, squid, and sea urchins. They also eat clams and abalone, a type of shellfish, by beating them against rocks to break open the shells.

- **Sharks**, killer whales, bears, coyotes, and eagles are the primary predators of sea otters.

- **Sea otters** are endangered. They have been regularly hunted for their thick fur, causing a steep decline in their numbers. Oil spills have also killed numerous sea otters.

Polar bears

✳ **Polar bears** are found in the Arctic region, along the icy northern shores of Russia, Greenland, and Canada.

✳ **They are the biggest** meat eaters, or carnivores, that live on land. Male polar bears are bigger than females and can weigh over 1,400 pounds.

✳ **Polar bears** are easily recognized by their thick white fur. The fur provides the bears with excellent camouflage in the snow. Underneath its fur, the polar bear's skin is dark.

▼ *Unlike other arctic mammals, the polar bear does not shed its coat in summer.*

🌟 **The fur is oily** and waterproof. The hair does not stick together when wet, allowing the animal to shake the water off its body.

🌟 **Polar bears** have small heads and slender necks. Their long, streamlined bodies make them excellent swimmers.

🌟 **Their front paws** are wide and help them paddle through water. Several tiny protrusions and suction pads under the paws give these animals a firm grip on the ice. They also use their front paws to stun prey.

🌟 **Polar bears** feed mainly on seals. They are also known to scavenge on the carcasses of whales and walruses.

🌟 **These animals** are skilled hunters. Sometimes they lie still on the edge of the ocean, waiting for a seal to surface. The moment the seal comes out, the polar bear pounces on it.

🌟 **In summer**, polar bears prefer to stalk their prey on land. While stalking, they sometimes lie on their chest with their rump in the air. They then lunge forward using their powerful hind legs, grabbing the seal before it escapes.

🌟 **Polar bears** often cover their black nose with their paws while waiting for prey. This helps them to blend in with the snow and remain unseen.

 # Exploration and travel

The first boats

Based on drawings and models found in Egypt, there is evidence that boats date back as far as 6000 BC. In fact, recent studies suggest that boats were common in Asia and Africa even before that.

Wood was the most popular material used to build boats in ancient times. In some ancient civilizations, such as Mesopotamia, boats were made of animal skin stretched over bones.

Later coracles, or round boats covered with animal skin, were developed. These boats had wicker frames and were used mainly for fishing.

Kayaks were another type of skin boat. They were used by the Inuit in Greenland for whaling. Kayaks are still used today, but mostly for recreation.

Dugouts soon replaced skin boats. At first, dugouts were merely hollowed-out tree trunks. Later these hollows were made watertight by either inserting a separate piece of wood, called a transom, on both ends, or by sealing the ends with clay.

The Egyptians built rafts by tying papyrus reeds together. These lightweight boats were used for fishing and for transporting light goods on the Nile. Later, the need to transport heavier cargo led the Egyptians to build stronger wooden boats.

DID YOU KNOW?

The Chinese made strong ships known as "junks." These ships had a number of large sails usually made of linen, and were steered by rudders, or movable blades on the stern. Junks were largely used to transport cargo. However, in several parts of China, they also served as houses and schools.

▼ In ancient Egypt, the first boats were made from bundles of papyrus reeds tied together. These boats did not last long but were easy to build.

* **Egyptian rafts** were made from planks of wood tied together. Unfortunately, they were not very sturdy and were used only for trips along rivers and coasts.

* **Sails** were gradually developed to harness wind energy and move boats at a greater speed. Sails were first developed by the Egyptians, who equipped their reed boats with square sails.

* **The Phoenicians** developed the sail further. They were mainly traders and needed to travel long distances. During the period from 1500 to 1000 BC, they developed excellent sailboats.

* **Shipbuilding** received a boost during the age of exploration, from AD 1000 to 1500. The Vikings and Portuguese and Spanish sailors went on long voyages, which required fast, sturdy, and dependable ships.

Ancient cargo ships

★ **In ancient Mesopotamia**, which is in modern-day Iraq, the earliest boats were of three types. These were wooden boats with triangular sails; tub-shaped boats called *guffa*, which were made from reeds and animal skins; and rafts made of timber and inflated animal skins, called *kalakku*.

★ **The *kalakku*** did not have sails. Instead, it relied on currents to float downstream. Once the boat reached its destination, the cargo was offloaded and the boat dismantled. It was then transported upstream on donkeys.

★ **Massive clay pots** were used as floats. Animal skins were stretched across the inner and outer surfaces of the pots to keep them waterproof.

★ **The earliest wooden boats** were simple structures. They were either pieces of log tied together or hollowed-out tree trunks. They could only carry a small amount of cargo.

★ **With the need to transport** more cargo, the simple wooden boats were modified. Sails were first developed in Egypt in about 3500 BC and were used in reed boats built to transport large stones.

★ **The invention of the sail** revolutionized shipbuilding, as it resulted in the ability to move big boat hulls. This allowed the transportation of large quantities of cargo at one time.

★ **The Phoenicians** were the most skilled shipbuilders of ancient times. They made huge merchant vessels with strong wooden hulls, capable of carrying large amounts of cargo.

⭐ **While most ancient boats** were small and were used to transport cargo down rivers, oceangoing vessels were being made in Asia.

⭐ **People of the Indus Valley civilization** are believed to have used ships to trade with other civilizations such as Mesopotamia, while Chinese cargo ships called "junks" are known to have traveled as far as Africa.

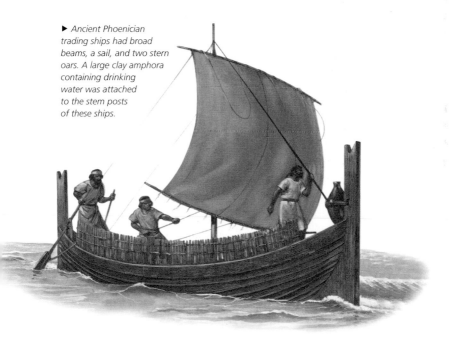

▶ Ancient Phoenician trading ships had broad beams, a sail, and two stern oars. A large clay amphora containing drinking water was attached to the stem posts of these ships.

Finding the way

★ **Marine navigation** involves guiding a boat or ship safely through the waters to its destination.

★ **In ancient times**, mariners stayed close to the shore so that they would not lose their way. In such instances, sailors used coastal navigation to determine their position. They kept in sight of land and used landmarks as reference points.

★ **When they finally** ventured into the open seas, these early seafarers depended on the positions of the sun, stars, and other celestial bodies to determine directions. Several instruments, including the sextant, were designed for this purpose.

★ **Modified versions** of some of the basic navigational tools from the past are still in use. The best known is the magnetic compass, which is crucial in determining direction at sea.

★ **A compass consists** of a moving needle that automatically points toward the earth's magnetic north. The instrument has been in use since the 12th century. The mariner's compass was an early form of the magnetic compass.

◄ A compass was used by the ship's captain to show his bearing, or direction.

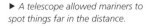
▶ A telescope allowed mariners to spot things far in the distance.

The mariner's compass consisted of an iron needle and a lodestone. The needle was rubbed against the lodestone, then stuck in a piece of straw and floated in a bowl of water. The needle would come to a rest pointing toward north.

Other primitive tools of navigation included the jackstaff. This instrument was used to measure the North Star's distance from the horizon and thus determine the position of the vessel at sea.

Ancient navigators also used a line with a piece of lead on one end to measure the depth of the water, thereby determining how far into the sea the vessel has sailed.

Dead reckoning was another popular method of determining the position of a vessel. For this, navigators calculate the ship's position, or the "fix," with its speed, time, and direction.

Nautical charts provided details about bodies of water, like the depth of the water and the location of islands, shores, rocks, and lighthouses.

DID YOU KNOW?
To calculate ship speed, early mariners dropped overboard a log tied to a reel of rope, knotted at regular intervals. The faster the ship traveled, the more the rope was unwound from the reel. The mariners counted the number of knots pulled off the reel in a given period of time and determined the speed of the ship in knots.

Viking voyagers

✦ **Vikings** came from the Scandinavian countries of Denmark, Sweden, and Norway. They were great travelers and spent much of their life at sea. They also invaded several countries.

✦ **The name "Viking"** means "pirate raid" in the Norse language. Although some Vikings were indeed pirates, most of them were farmers who sailed from their countries in search of better agricultural lands.

✦ **Their passion** for sailing made the Vikings the best shipbuilders of their time. They built two kinds of ships, the longship and the *knarr*, also called *knórr*.

▼ *Viking ships are believed to be the first vessels to have crossed the Atlantic Ocean. The Vikings discovered Iceland around AD 860 and settled in the new land.*

* **The longship** was a long and narrow vessel, mainly used as a warship. On average the longship was 100 feet long, and was powered by a single, square sail. Made of sheep's wool or linen, the sails often cost more than the rest of the ship.

* **Viking women** were responsible for making the sails. They first made small, diamond-shaped pieces and trimmed them with leather strips. These pieces were then sewn together to make a large, square sail.

* **The *knórr*** was a heavy cargo ship. It was about 55 feet long and wider than the longship. It was used to carry cargo, such as wool, timber, grain, and even livestock.

* **When building a ship**, the Vikings first erected the keel, a large beam around which the hull of the ship was built. The keel ran the entire length of the ship, from the bow to the stern, and was made of a single piece of wood.

    * **Wooden planks** were affixed to the sides of the keel in an overlapping pattern. The planks were then fastened with iron nails. This technique made the ships sturdy and flexible. The floor was set on the keel, and bars were put across to make a deck and seats for oarsmen. The ships were steered by oars at the stern.

        * **The bow** of the longship sometimes had an ornate carving of a snake or a dragon head. These ships, therefore, were often referred to as "dragon ships" by the Vikings' enemies.

Erik the Red

- **Erik the Red**, born in AD 950 in Jaeren, Norway, was one of the first European explorers to reach North America. He was born Erik Thorvaldson but, due to his red hair, was called Erik the Red.

- **When Erik** was a little boy, his father, Thorvald, was exiled on charges of murder. They left Norway and settled in Iceland.

- **Around 982**, Erik was banned from Iceland for three years for manslaughter. During this time he explored Greenland, which had been discovered by his fellow countryman, Gunnbjorn Ulfsson, almost 50 years before.

- **After his three-year exile**, Erik returned to Iceland to tell stories about the new land he named Greenland. He then sailed back to Greenland with several other Vikings who joined him to settle in this new land.

- **Erik's son**, Leif Eriksson, was born around 980. He is popularly known as "Leif the Lucky." Like his father, Leif also was a great seafarer.

- **Leif** was only 24 years old when he led his first voyage. On this trip, he sailed to Norway carrying gifts for King Olaf. When he landed in Norway, Leif was invited to be the king's guest.

- **During his stay**, Leif learned about Christianity and adopted the religion. He also took a priest back with him to Greenland in order to spread the message of Christianity.

- **As a boy**, Leif had heard of a trader, Bjarni Herjolfsson, who claimed he sighted a new land to the southwest of Greenland. After his return from Norway, Leif set sail in search of Bjarni's land.

* **On his way**, Leif landed on Baffin Island in present-day Canada. He named it Helluland, which meant "flat rock land." From there he traveled south to Labrador, finally arriving at the land Bjarni had spoken about.

* **Leif named this new land** Vinland, meaning "Wineland," after discovering grapes on this land. The remains of a Vinland settlement can be seen at L'Anse aux Meadows in Newfoundland, Canada.

▼ *The Vikings were great seafarers and consequently traveled to many different lands.*

287

Marco Polo

Marco Polo is one of the most famous explorers in history. He was born in Venice, Italy, in 1254 and died in 1324.

He was the first European to travel across the entire Asian continent and reach China. He later published a popular book entitled *The Travels of Marco Polo*.

Marco Polo's father, Niccolo, and his uncle, Maffeo, were great explorers too. In 1260, the two men set off on their first journey to China, where they met Kublai Khan, the Mongol emperor.

Around 1269, the Polo brothers returned to Italy. However, toward the end of 1271, the brothers once again embarked on another journey to China. This time, Marco Polo accompanied them.

◀ *It is believed that Marco Polo governed the city of Yangzhou during his stay in China.*

- **At first**, they planned to take the sea route from the Persian Gulf to China. However, the ships available were not good enough, so they decided to travel by land.

- **On their way**, the trio crossed Afghanistan and the Pamir Mountains, before taking the Silk Road to China.

DID YOU KNOW?
Some historians doubt Marco Polo's journey, since his journals do not contain any mention of the Great Wall and common Chinese customs such as the use of chopsticks.

- **During his long journey**, Marco Polo recorded all that he saw. He also gave a detailed account of the rise of the Mongols and the life of Kublai Khan.

- **Finally**, three and a half years after they left Venice, the Polos arrived at Cambaluc, the capital of the Mongol empire. The trio had traveled a grueling 5,500 miles to reach their destination.

- **Marco Polo** was impressed with the Chinese, their means of communication, and their use of paper money and coal. In fact, he was so involved with the matters of the emperor that Marco Polo spent 17 years in the court of Kublai Khan before finally returning home.

- **Marco Polo** opted for the sea route on his return journey. He sailed through the South China Sea and the Indian Ocean. Several of his crew members died during the voyage, probably of scurvy or malaria.

Bartolomeu Dias

⭐ **Bartolomeu Dias** (*c*. 1450–1500) was a Portuguese explorer who traveled to the unexplored shores of Africa. Little is known about his birth and childhood.

⭐ **Portugal** was one of the foremost seafaring countries in Europe during the 15th century. The king often commissioned voyages in search of new lands. In 1486, King John II sent Dias on a voyage to find a trade route around Africa leading to Asia.

⭐ **After ten months** of preparation, Dias finally set sail from Lisbon, the capital of Portugal, in August 1487. He took two caravels, or sailboats, and one supply ship.

⭐ **Dias took with him** six Africans who could convey the Portuguese king's goodwill to the native people. They were also to convey the king's message of peace and his wish to meet Prester John, the king of Ethiopia.

⭐ **In 1488**, Dias became the first European to sail around Cape Agulhas, the southernmost tip of Africa.

⭐ **On February 3, 1488**, Dias landed at Mossel Bay, located to the east of the Cape of Good Hope. He carried on until he reached the Indian Ocean by sea, a discovery that also opened a sea route to India.

⭐ **During this journey**, Dias sighted the Cape of Good Hope. He originally named it Cabo Tormentoso, meaning "Cape of Storms."

⭐ **According to a legend**, King John renamed it Cabo da boa Esperanca, or the Cape of Good Hope, since it opened up a world of commercial opportunities.

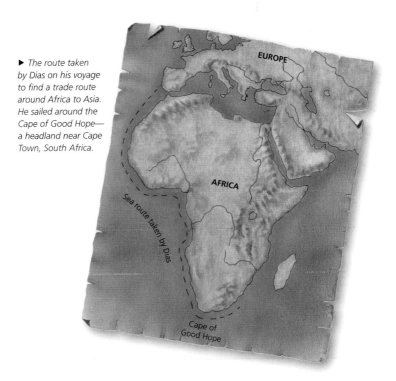

▶ The route taken by Dias on his voyage to find a trade route around Africa to Asia. He sailed around the Cape of Good Hope—a headland near Cape Town, South Africa.

EUROPE

AFRICA

Sea route taken by Dias

Cape of Good Hope

In 1497, Dias accompanied the Portuguese explorer Vasco da Gama on the latter's expedition to India. He followed da Gama up to the Cape Verde Islands, where he left the expedition at Sao Jorge de Mina, the Portuguese fortress on the Gold Coast, present-day Ghana.

Christopher Columbus

★ **Christopher Columbus** (1451–1506) was an Italian explorer who sailed across the Atlantic Ocean to establish a westward sea route to Asia. Instead, this great mariner landed in the Americas.

★ **Columbus** was only 14 years old when he first set out to sea. He worked on various ships and even led voyages to Tunisia and Anjou in Africa.

★ **After settling in Portugal** for a few years, Columbus moved to Spain with his son. Columbus was driven by a passion for exploring new lands. He made repeated pleas to the Spanish monarchs to fund his expeditions.

★ **Initially**, Columbus received no support. The Christian rulers of Spain were more concerned with battling the Moorish kingdom of Granada than with funding overseas exploration. However, once victory against Granada was certain, they became more receptive.

★ **Columbus** once again approached King Ferdinand and Queen Isabella of Spain. This time he convinced them that he would find a trade route to the Far East.

★ **On August 3, 1492**, the Italian mariner finally set sail from Palos, Spain, with three ships, the *Niña*, *Pinta*, and *Santa Maria*. The ships carried over 100 men, ship-repairing equipment, and supplies.

★ **After sailing** for five long months, Columbus and his crew sighted land. They set foot on an island that they thought was in Asia. But it was actually a part of the Bahamas. Columbus named this island San Salvador.

▲ *The* Santa Maria *was wrecked when it ran into rocks off the coast of present-day Haiti. Its remains were used to build a fort on the island.*

Columbus continued his journey to Cuba, Haiti, and the Dominican Republic. He named the natives "Indians," since he thought that he was, in fact, in the Indies.

On March 15, 1493, Columbus returned to Spain, where he was accorded a hero's welcome. He was given the title of Admiral of the Ocean Seas and made the governor of all the lands he had discovered.

Amerigo Vespuccia

⭐ **The continents** of North and South America were named after the Italian explorer Amerigo Vespucci.

⭐ **Vespucci** was born in Florence, Italy, in 1454. Even as a boy, Vespucci was interested in geography, the study of stars and the exploration of new lands.

⭐ **He was the first** to dispute Columbus's claim that he had landed in a part of Asia. Instead, Vespucci firmly believed that the landmass discovered was a "new world" and not in Asia.

▼ *An early map of the Americas. Vespucci was not the first European to sight these continents, but he was the first to identify the New World as separate from Asia.*

★ **In 1492**, Vespucci left Florence. He settled in Seville, Spain, where he became the director of a shipping company that provided resources for the expeditions of Columbus.

★ **Vespucci** is said to have obtained the support of King Ferdinand of Spain for an expedition and set sail in 1497. Although little is known about this voyage, it is believed that he must have sailed along the coasts of Mexico and North America.

★ **In 1499**, Vespucci embarked on a second voyage. This was the first planned voyage to the Americas. During this trip Vespucci explored the northeastern coast of South America and also landed in Cuba and the Bahamas.

★ **In 1501**, he led another expedition to the Americas, this time funded by King Manuel I of Portugal. Although this voyage was not as successful as the others, Vespucci still managed to discover parts of Brazil.

★ **In 1503**, Vespucci went farther south along the South American coast and spotted the Falkland Islands, off Argentina.

★ **Vespucci** was one of the earliest explorers to describe South America as a continent. In his accounts published in 1507, the terms "New World" and "America" were first used with reference to the lands Vespucci visited.

★ **Vespucci made maps** of coastal South America that were sold to a German cartographer. According to one theory, the maps were reproduced with Vespucci's name on the map. People thought this was the name of the land, and it came to be called America.

Vasco da Gama

★ **Vasco da Gama** (*c.* 1460–1524) was a Portuguese explorer who discovered a sea route to India.

★ **In 1488**, Bartolomeu Dias had opened up the possibilities of a new route to the East by discovering the southern tip of Africa. He established that India could be reached by water, but his work was only half done.

★ **Arab traders** held the monopoly of trade with the Eastern countries at that time. In order to outflank them, King João II of Portugal commissioned Estevão da Gama, Vasco's father, to complete Dias's journey.

★ **Estevão** died before he could complete the voyage. Moreover, a shortage of funds put an end to further Portuguese expeditions for a brief period.

★ **Following the death** of King João II in 1495, his cousin, King Manuel I, ascended the throne of Portugal. King Manuel I decided to renew João's efforts to reach the East and put Vasco da Gama in charge of the expedition.

★ **Vasco da Gama** planned his journey thoroughly and stocked four ships with supplies. He was accompanied by Goncalo Alvares, his brother Paolo da Gama, and his companion Nicolao Coelho, who often sailed with Vasco da Gama.

★ **On July 8, 1497**, da Gama set sail from Lisbon. His crew consisted of 170 men, many of whom were convicts.

🟊 **By December**, Vasco da Gama's fleet had reached the southernmost part of Africa. From there, the fleet continued to sail along the east coast of Africa.

🟊 **Vasco da Gama** stopped at coastal towns like Mozambique and Mombasa to replenish his stocks. Throughout his journey he faced opposition from Arab traders. Vasco, however, met an Arab guide at Malindi, in what is now Kenya. The guide agreed to lead the Portuguese across the Arabian Sea.

🟊 **On May 20, 1498**, Vasco da Gama finally reached the Indian port of Calicut, which was then the main trading center for spices and precious stones.

▶ *In 1524, Vasco da Gama was made the Portuguese viceroy to India and he set off on his third and final voyage. This great explorer, however, died soon after arriving in the city of Cochin, India.*

297

Ferdinand Magellan

Ferdinand Magellan was born in 1480, into a noble Portuguese family. He led the first sea voyage around the globe. He was also the first European to cross the Pacific Ocean.

Like Columbus, Magellan believed that a westward sea passage to Asia existed. He also realized that he would need to cross the New World, or the Americas.

Having fallen out of favor with the Portuguese monarch, Magellan gave up his nationality and left for Spain. There, he met with King Charles I and told him of his plans to approach the Spice Islands in Asia from the west.

The king granted him funds and on September 20, 1519, Magellan set sail with a fleet of five ships and over 200 men. He sailed along the coast of Africa toward Brazil.

◀ Magellan's journey not only proved that the earth was round, but also showed that the oceans of the world were linked.

- **On December 6**, Magellan sighted Brazil. After stocking up on supplies at Rio de Janeiro, the crew continued down the coast of South America toward the Pacific Ocean.

- **Finally**, in October 1520, they found a strait. Magellan named it the Strait of All Saints. Later this strait was renamed the Strait of Magellan.

- **Conditions** in the strait were so difficult that one of the ships turned back. It took the remaining ships nearly 40 days to cross the narrow strait. At night, the crew saw an island where fires from Indian camps glowed through the dark. The crew named this island Tierra del Fuego, meaning "land of fire."

- **It took the fleet** four months to cross the Pacific Ocean. During this time, members of the crew suffered because of the lack of food and fresh water. Many came down with scurvy. Finally, the fleet arrived at the island of Guam in the South Pacific, where it managed to stock up on supplies.

- **The crew** continued to sail. On March 28, 1521, they reached the Philippines, where Magellan was killed in a tribal war. However, his crew carried on with the voyage under the leadership of Sebastian del Cano, one of Magellan's most skilled navigators.

- **On May 1, 1521**, Sebastian del Cano arrived at the Moluccas, or the Spice Islands. After stocking up on valuable spices, del Cano and his men started on their return voyage. Finally, on September 6, 1522, one ship carrying 18 crew members arrived in Spain, becoming the first to circumnavigate the globe.

Sir Francis Drake

Englishman Sir Francis Drake (c. 1540–1596) was a skilled navigator. His remarkable achievements demonstrated the growing power of the English navy, which was competing with Spain and Portugal to gain a monopoly over international trade.

Drake commanded his first ship in 1567 and traveled to the Caribbean on a slave-trading mission. During this expedition his fleet was ruthlessly attacked by the Spaniards. After suffering huge losses, Drake set out to replenish the stolen goods.

▼ *Queen Elizabeth I visited Drake aboard the* Golden Hind *and knighted him for his efforts.*

- **In 1572**, Drake led another expedition. On reaching the Isthmus of Panama, the land linking the Atlantic and Pacific oceans, Drake became the first Englishman to see the Pacific Ocean. He also led journeys to the Caribbean, attacking the Spanish ports there.

- **In 1577**, Drake was secretly sent by Queen Elizabeth I to capture the Spanish colonies on the western coast of the Americas. He set sail with five ships on December 13.

- **Drake** did not reveal the intended destination to his crew. When he turned south from Brazil, he faced opposition from his crew.

- **At Rio de la Plata** in present day-Argentina, Drake disposed of two unfit ships. He also gave a remarkable speech to cheer up his crew, and renamed his ship the *Golden Hind*.

- **The journey** proved to be difficult. When the fleet entered the Pacific Ocean after crossing the dangerous strait between the South American landmass and Tierra del Fuego, a violent storm destroyed one ship. Another turned back to England.

- **Drake**, however, did not give up. He continued to sail north, hoping to find a passage through the Americas. It is believed that Drake must have crossed California and reached the United States–Canada border.

- **Unable to find** a passage through the Americas, Drake turned west toward the Pacific Ocean. He visited the Moluccas, Celebes, Java, and finally the Cape of Good Hope. When he returned to England in September 1580, he became the first Englishman to have sailed around the world.

Voyages to Australia

European sailors might have found a sea route to the East through the Pacific Ocean. But it was not until the late 1600s that they discovered Australia and New Zealand. However, the maps made after 1540 indicated that a "southern land" did indeed exist.

It is believed that Chinese traders were in contact with the native inhabitants of this southern land, which we now know as Australia.

Arabs, too, are believed to have traded with the natives, later known as Aborigines, in north Australia.

Willem Jansz, a Dutch explorer, was the first European to sight Australia. In 1606, he sailed along 200 miles of the Australian coast, all the time believing that it was an extension of New Guinea. He called the land Nieu Zelandt. This name was not adopted. However, another Dutch explorer, Abel Janszoon Tasman, later used it to name New Zealand.

The first known landing took place in 1616. This time another Dutchman, named Dirk Hartog, landed on the west coast of Australia after his ship was blown off course en route to Java.

In 1642, Abel Tasman explored the southern coast and sighted the island of Tasmania, which was later named after him.

William Dampier, a pirate, was the first Englishman to land in Australia. He explored the northern and western coasts.

Captain James Cook was sent by British royalty in 1768 to discover the east coast of Australia. Sailing on the *Endeavour*, he went around the north coast and then sailed along the east coast.

🌟 **Cook made a map** of the east coast and discovered and named Botany Bay on the southeast of the island continent.

🌟 **In 1786**, the British government decided to colonize Australia. On May 13, 1787, Captain Arthur Phillip of the British Royal Navy set sail for Botany Bay with more than 1,000 people, mostly convicts. On January 26, 1788, Captain Phillip established the first European settlement in Port Jackson, what is now Sydney, in Australia. Although the Aborigines initially opposed it, the colonization of Australia was complete by the second half of the 19th century.

▶ As well as studying the planets, Cook took wildlife experts with him on his explorations. They collected plants that weren't known in Europe, and drew sketches and made notes about them.

Maori land

⭐ **Dutch explorer** Abel Tasman (1603–1659) was sent on a mission in 1642 to find the unknown "southern land," referred to as Terra Australis Incognita. It was believed that this land extended across the Pacific Ocean.

⭐ **On August 14, 1642**, Tasman began his journey from Batavia, present-day Jakarta in Indonesia. After reaching Mauritius, Tasman sailed east, missing Australia completely. In December 1642, he finally spotted the land we now know as Tasmania.

⭐ **Tasman named the island** Van Diemen's Land at the time. It was only later that the British colonists changed the name in honor of the explorer.

⭐ **After investigating** the island, Tasman continued his voyage farther east and discovered New Zealand. He named it Staten Landt, thinking that it was connected to a land located near the southern tip of South America.

⭐ **Tasman** looked for a bay to moor his ship, but faced opposition from the Maoris, the natives of New Zealand. He lost four of his crew members in this encounter.

⭐ **In 1766**, British explorer Captain James Cook had set sail to Tahiti in the *Endeavour* to observe the movement of the planet Venus in the sky. He also had a secret mission—to find the unknown southern land. He sailed south with the Tahitian chief Tupaia.

⭐ **In 1769**, Cook reached New Zealand and claimed it for the British Empire. Gradually, settlers from Great Britain started moving to New Zealand.

▲ *The Maoris were the first settlers of New Zealand. They are believed to have sailed all the way from Polynesia about 1,000 years ago.*

Other Europeans and Americans also arrived in New Zealand to make it a base for whaling and sealing. Missionaries followed to preach Christianity.

The early settlers faced resistance from the Maoris. In February 1840, they signed the Treaty of Waitangi to settle land disputes, but a battle erupted in 1860. With this, the colonization of New Zealand began.

The Maoris could not match the firepower of the settlers, whom they called *Pakehas*. Their defeat marked the beginning of European domination.

305

Cook's mission

⭐ **James Cook** was born on October 27, 1728, in Yorkshire, England. He was famous for his voyages in the Pacific Ocean and is credited with the discovery of the Hawaiian Islands.

⭐ **In 1755**, Cook joined Great Britain's Royal Navy. Soon after, the Royal Society of London chose Lieutenant Cook to lead a scientific voyage to the Pacific island of Tahiti.

⭐ **The mission** involved the observation of a rare astronomical phenomenon, the passing of the planet Venus between the earth and the sun. It was believed that this would help scientists calculate the distance between the earth and the sun.

⭐ **There was another motive** behind the voyage. The British Empire wanted to gain more information about Australia, a continent that had been sighted by Abel Tasman.

DID YOU KNOW?
Fearing an outbreak of scurvy among his crew, Cook fed them citrus fruits, carrots, and marmalade. Later, it was discovered that citrus fruits, rich in vitamin C, help prevent scurvy.

⭐ **Cook set sail** from Plymouth on the *Endeavour*. On April 11, 1769, Cook and his team of scientists reached Tahiti after sailing around South America. They observed the movements of Venus from there.

⭐ **He then sailed** in search of the southern land and reached New Zealand. On his return, he sailed along the eastern coast of Australia. Back home in England, Cook was commended for his achievements and made a naval commander.

▶ *Captain James Cook's historic ship the* Endeavour *was built in 1764 in Yorkshire, England. The ship was originally named the* Earl of Pembroke *and was first used to transport coal.*

★ **Cook's** second voyage was more ambitious. Having concluded that neither New Zealand nor Australia was a part of the southern continent, Cook set off in search of this elusive land.

★ **On January 17, 1773,** Cook became the first to cross the Antarctic Circle. Although Cook had sailed farther south than any other explorer, he never sighted land. However, he did discover a group of islands in the Pacific, which were later named the Cook Islands.

★ **On his third voyage,** Cook wanted to prove the existence of the Northwest Passage, which was thought to exist as a link between the Pacific and Atlantic oceans. During this journey, he discovered the Hawaiian Islands. He named them the Sandwich Islands after his friend, the Earl of Sandwich.

★ **Initially the natives** gave Cook and his crew a warm welcome. But their trust soon wore off, and they became hostile toward the foreigners. On February 14, 1779, Cook was stabbed to death by the natives.

In search of El Dorado

⭐ **El Dorado**, a Spanish term meaning "the golden one," was probably first used by 16th-century Spanish explorers to describe a legendary golden city in South America.

⭐ **Stories of the vast wealth** of this city reached Europe, and Spanish explorers were determined to find it.

⭐ **It was believed** that whenever a new ruler was appointed to the Chibcha tribe of South America, his entire body was covered with gold dust. He then washed it off in a sacred lake, called Guatavita.

⭐ **It was also thought** that the chosen leader threw a pile of gold and other precious stones into the lake. In the legends, the city was also referred to as Manoa.

⭐ **According to a recent theory**, the city was called Paititi by the Incas. It is believed that when the Spaniards invaded their land in 1532, the Incas fled to Paititi with their treasures.

◀ *It is believed that Sir Walter Raleigh first heard about El Dorado from Pedro Sarmiento de Gamboa, a famous Spanish explorer of the 16th century.*

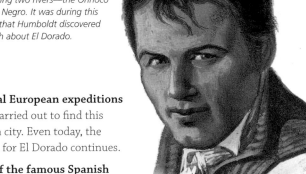

▶ *Alexander von Humboldt was the first to sail down the Casiquiare Canal, the only natural canal connecting two rivers—the Orinoco and the Negro. It was during this voyage that Humboldt discovered the truth about El Dorado.*

Several European expeditions were carried out to find this golden city. Even today, the search for El Dorado continues.

One of the famous Spanish voyages in search of El Dorado was that of Diego de Ordaz around 1531. In 1541, another famous Spanish adventurer, Francisco de Orellana, sailed down the Amazon River in search of the fabled city.

At the same time, Philip von Hutten, a German explorer, also tried his luck. Although each explorer had a tale to tell, none of these voyages could conclusively prove the existence of El Dorado.

In 1595, Sir Walter Raleigh, a British explorer, embarked on a similar mission. He returned and declared that Manoa was a city on Lake Parima in Guiana, present-day Venezuela.

German naturalist and explorer Alexander von Humboldt finally dismissed this myth of a land of gold on a lake.

Finding the North Pole

★ **The North Pole** lies in the frozen waters of the Arctic Ocean. Its ice sheet shifts during very heavy snowstorms. This makes any expedition to the North Pole extremely difficult.

★ **American explorer Admiral Robert E. Peary** (1856–1920) and his companion Matthew Henson understood the perils of an expedition to the North Pole. They made repeated trips to the region to assess the problems they might face.

★ **Peary spent time** among the Inuit of Greenland, learning their way of life.

★ **When he realized** that the North Pole was not a part of Greenland, and that it was farther north, Peary chose Ellesmere Island in Canada as the starting point for the expedition.

★ **Peary and his companion** had failed to reach the North Pole on two earlier attempts, but the lessons they learned during these trips proved invaluable and eventually led to their success.

★ **The route** to the North Pole is especially difficult because ships cannot get close due to the ice sheets. Walking is not easy either, as the ice pack is full of pressure ridges and crevices.

★ **The ship Peary used** for the expedition was called the *Roosevelt*. He designed it so that it was capable of crushing through the ice to reach as far north as possible. He took several Inuit to help with the expedition.

★ **About 475 miles** from the North Pole, the crew set up their winter base camp and began to prepare for the final part of the expedition.

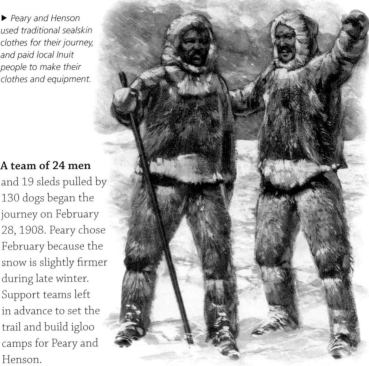

▶ Peary and Henson used traditional sealskin clothes for their journey, and paid local Inuit people to make their clothes and equipment.

A team of 24 men and 19 sleds pulled by 130 dogs began the journey on February 28, 1908. Peary chose February because the snow is slightly firmer during late winter. Support teams left in advance to set the trail and build igloo camps for Peary and Henson.

About 150 miles from the North Pole, Peary, Henson, and four Inuit left the last support team to make the final dash with the best dogs and light sleds. They had good weather, and the team finally reached the North Pole on April 6, 1909.

Exploring Antarctica

✴ **Norwegian explorer** Roald Amundsen (1872–1928) was no stranger to the polar regions. After two successful expeditions to Antarctica and the Northwest Passage in the north, Amundsen made plans to go to the Arctic.

✴ **In April 1909**, Robert E. Peary became the first man to reach the North Pole. Upon hearing this news, Amundsen immediately turned his attention to the South Pole.

✴ **British explorer** Robert F. Scott also began his expedition to the South Pole at the same time.

✴ **Amundsen**, who wanted to be the first to reach the South Pole, chose a different route when he set off in his ship, the *Fram*. His crew members were unaware of the change of route for a month.

✴ **On January 14, 1911**, Amundsen and his crew arrived at the Bay of Whales on the Ross Ice Shelf, where they set up their winter base camp. Throughout the winter, Amundsen and his team prepared for their journey.

DID YOU KNOW?
In 1926, 15 years after first setting foot on the South Pole, Amundsen became the first person to fly over the North Pole, in an airship called the Norge.

✴ **On October 20, 1911**, after several initial setbacks, a team of five men eventually set off for the South Pole. Each traveled on a sled pulled by 13 dogs.

✴ **Meanwhile**, Scott was facing problems. He had taken ponies instead of dogs to haul sleds. The ponies soon became exhausted and were unable to go on.

▶ *Amundsen arrived at the South Pole 35 days before Scott. He left a letter addressed to Scott to show him that he had got there first.*

Scott's winter camp was set up at McMurdo Sound, which was almost 60 miles farther from the South Pole than the Bay of Whales.

Amundsen and his team took a mountainous route that was almost 10,000 feet high. He named the mountains Queen Maud's Range, after the queen of Norway. At the summit, the party had to slaughter a few of their dogs to feed the other ones.

The team persevered despite a searing blizzard. Their final obstacle was the Devil's Ballroom, a thin crust of snow covering a number of crevasses.

After braving frostbite and exhaustion for almost two months, Amundsen finally reached the South Pole on December 14, 1911.

313

Sailing ships

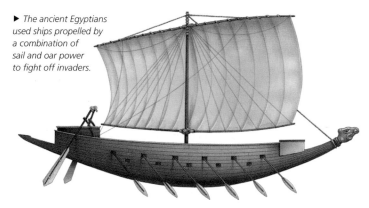

▶ The ancient Egyptians used ships propelled by a combination of sail and oar power to fight off invaders.

⭐ **Sailing ships** use the energy of the wind to move. A sail is made up of pieces of cloth stitched together and tied to long poles called masts.

⭐ **Egyptians** are believed to have first developed sails. Their reed boats were simple, flat-bottomed structures with a huge square sail. Since these vessels did not have a keel, the mast was attached to the edge, or gunwale, of the boat.

⭐ **The Phoenicians**, during the period 1500–1000 BC, modified the sailboats further. They also created a small space in the hull, called the deck, to protect sailors from bad weather.

⭐ **New sailing vessels** were developed for use at war. These were known as galleys and had rows of oarsmen as well as sails. These gave way to the bireme, a big vessel that had two decks of oarsmen, followed by the trireme.

⭐ **In China**, shipbuilders built a superior cargo boat called the junk. This boat had a number of sails and was steered by rudders, or movable blades on the stern.

⭐ **The Vikings** developed the longship, which was later replaced by 13th-century cargo vessels, called cogs, as the major carrier of goods in Europe.

⭐ **In the 15th century**, sturdy boats called caravels were made in Spain and Portugal. They had four sails and were up to 80 feet long.

⭐ **Galleons** had long, slender hulls and were quite fast. The Spanish armada used this vessel. The famous *Mayflower*, which took the Pilgrims to America in 1620, was a galleon.

⭐ **With the British Empire** beginning to expand in the 19th century, ships became larger and more fortified. They often carried riches back from India and Africa.

⭐ **The advent of steamships** gradually led to the demise of sailing ships. Sailing is now a leisure activity, and sailboats are used for cruising, racing, or fishing.

▶ *Sir Francis Drake took three years to sail around the world in his favorite ship, the* Golden Hind.

315

Ships and boats today

★ **Modern ships** and boats are highly developed when compared to those used in ancient times. Today, we have a wide choice of ships and boats suited for all purposes, from pleasure boats to cargo ships and battleships.

★ **Sailboats** of the past have given way to sophisticated fuel-driven vessels. Iron, steel, and fiberglass hulls have replaced wooden hulls to provide greater speed and durability.

▼ *This luxury powerboat has a motor engine that enables it to travel at high speeds.*

✦ **Modern commercial ships** are of various types. However, they are broadly classified into cargo and passenger ships. Cargo ships are used to transport goods, while passenger liners carry people.

✦ **Among the different kinds** of cargo ships, tankers are most widely used. These ships are used to transport crude oil, gas, or chemicals, and are the largest oceangoing vessels.

✦ **Reefers**, or refrigerated container ships, are used for transporting perishable goods, such as fruit, vegetables, and meat.

✦ **Boats**, too, are of different types. These include high-speed jet boats, motorboats, iceboats, rowboats, and sailboats.

✦ **Oars and sails** are still extremely popular. However, motorboats are more common now. These vessels have an internal-combustion engine that provides both speed and power.

✦ **Modern navies** have a variety of warships. These include cruisers, destroyers, aircraft carriers, frigates, and various support vessels.

✦ **Our knowledge** of marine life and resources depends heavily on research vessels. Fitted with state-of-the-art equipment, these ships undertake study expeditions.

✦ **Specialized ships** and boats are used for fishing, patrolling, repairing, and rescue operations. Sophisticated vessels like trawlers, long-liners, seiners, and lobster boats that use a variety of fishing gear have replaced old wooden fishing boats.

Modern navigation

⭐ **The navigation equipment** used in the early days of seafaring has undergone a major change. Electronic navigation has replaced manual techniques, and advanced high-tech gadgets are now being used worldwide.

⭐ **Modern navigational tools** are more accurate than ancient, manual methods. Some of the most important inventions are radio direction finding, long-ranging navigation, and radar.

⭐ **One of the first forms** of radio navigation was radio direction finding, or RDF. With this method, navigators tuned in to a particular radio frequency to determine their position. Some specific signals also had their own Morse code.

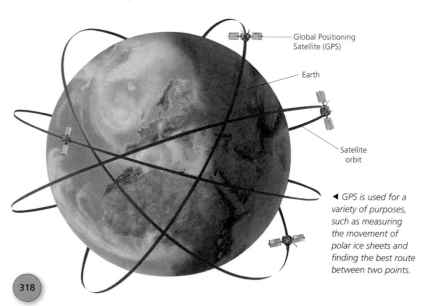

Global Positioning Satellite (GPS)

Earth

Satellite orbit

◀ *GPS is used for a variety of purposes, such as measuring the movement of polar ice sheets and finding the best route between two points.*

⭐ **Long-range navigation**, or loran, helps to fix the position of the ship by measuring the time taken by different radio signals to reach the receiver from fixed onshore transmitters.

⭐ **The most popular form** of loran is loran-C, which uses two land transmitters simultaneously. This system is now being replaced by the Global Positioning System, or GPS.

⭐ **GPS is a type of modern** satellite navigation, or satellite positioning system. This process uses 24 artificial satellites orbiting the earth, the first of which was launched in the early 21st century.

⭐ **With this system**, the navigator has a GPS receiver. A control device keeps track of the satellites, which send signals and the exact time. Comparing data from more than one satellite, the receiver calculates the ship's exact position.

⭐ **The traditional** dead-reckoning system (DRS) has been modified into the inertial guidance system. This has the same function as the earlier DRS, but is more accurate.

⭐ **Radio detection and ranging**, popularly called radar, is another commonly used navigational technique. Radar helps to locate faraway objects by bouncing radio waves off them.

⭐ **A radar uses a scanner** to determine the location of objects, and has a display that shows its findings. It can not only locate the presence and position of an object, it can also determine its shape, size, speed, and direction of movement.

Modern cargo ships

★ **Cargo ships**, also called freighters, are usually huge and are used to transport cargo such as cars, trucks, food products, oil, textiles, minerals, gas, and metals.

★ **Cargo ships** that have fixed routes and charges are known as liners. Tramps are ships that do not operate on any definite route or schedule. These vessels arrive at any port where cargo is available.

★ **There are two main kinds** of cargo ships—container ships and bulk carriers. Tankers and supertankers are also cargo ships, but are considered a separate category due to the nature of their cargo.

★ **Container ships** carry their cargo in large containers. They are sometimes referred to as "box boats." These ships carry all kinds of dry cargo, from computers and televisions to furniture and foodstuffs.

★ **Bulk carriers** are single-deck vessels that are used to carry unpackaged, free-flowing dry cargo such as grain, ore, and coal. These ships have one large container or space. Products such as grain and coal are poured into this large container through openings in its roof.

★ **Small container ships** called coasters carry small amounts of cargo from minor ports to major ports. They are also known as feeder vessels, since they "feed" cargo to bigger container ships.

★ **Coasters** are named for the fact that they travel along the coast. These ships usually make more than one stop per trip.

* **Roll-on-roll-off**, or RORO vessels, and lighter aboard ships, or LASH, are popular alternatives to container ships. RORO ships have openings on their sides and stern, or the back of the ship, through which cars, trucks, and even wheeled containers can be driven aboard.

* **The LASH vessel** is also called a barge carrier. It is a long cargo ship with a crane mounted on its deck. In this system, cargo is placed in flat-bottomed boats, or barges, that are loaded into a mother ship, or LASH carrier.

* **The vessel** can load or offload several barges near a port and move on without wasting time. Barges that have been left behind are towed into the docks and unloaded at leisure.

▼ With the advent of container ships, huge cranes became a standard feature at cargo ship docks. Some cargo ships have onboard cranes called derricks. Cranes and derricks speed up the process of loading and unloading cargo.

Tankers

✦ **Tankers** are huge ships used for transporting petroleum or natural gas. Some tankers also carry chemicals.

✦ **All countries** depend on oil and oil products, but few have these natural resources. Oil therefore needs to be transported from oil-rich countries to other parts of the world.

✦ **Oil pipelines** and tankers are the only modes of transporting oil around the world. Tankers are, in fact, one or more tanks designed like a ship.

✦ **Tankers are divided** into various groups depending on the nature of their cargo. The different types of tankers include liquid natural gas (LNG) carriers, very large crude carriers (VLCC), ultra large crude carriers (ULCC), medium-range carriers, Suezmax, and Panamax.

✦ **The largest** of all tankers are the supertankers. They are alternatively known as VLCCs or ULCCs. These tankers are about 1,300 feet long and mainly carry crude oil.

✦ **Supertankers** are even bigger than aircraft carriers, making them the biggest ships in the world. Since they are too large to approach most ports, these ships often have to unload their cargo into smaller vessels. Today, however, some ports have deep-water unloading facilities that are connected to the mainland by pipelines.

★ **Tankers** carry millions of gallons of oil. Even the smallest accident can cause the oil to spill and result in extensive damage to the environment. Hence, tankers require extremely strong hulls to prevent such accidents.

★ **Tankers with single hulls** are at the most risk, since the hull is also the wall of the oil tank. A breach in the hull would lead to a major oil spill.

★ **Double-hulled tankers** are considered safer because there is a space between the hull and the oil tanks. Very few oil tankers, however, have double hulls.

★ **Tankers** also have sophisticated firefighting equipment, along with modern pumps to load and unload their liquid cargo.

▶ *This tanker is carrying liquid petroleum. Some tankers have caused huge environmental damage through oil spills and other accidents.*

323

Container ships

⭐ **In the 1950s**, Malcom McLean, an American trucker, came up with an alternative for the time-consuming and expensive process of manually loading and unloading cargo.

⭐ **McLean** suggested that ships be loaded with big, ready-made containers. These containers would be filled with cargo and lifted by cranes onto ships directly from trucks.

▼ Cargo is loaded onto container ships by huge cranes that can lift 20–30 containers per hour.

★ **This process** of using containers to carry cargo is called "containerization." It is believed that the idea struck McLean while waiting for the cargo from his truck to be loaded onto a ship.

★ **Container shipping** integrated the movement of goods from trucks, trains, ships, and even planes. Today, almost 90 percent of the world's cargo is moved in containers.

★ **The first container ship** was the *Ideal X*, which sailed from New Jersey in 1956. The world's first terminal exclusively for containers was constructed in Port Elizabeth, New Jersey.

★ **OOCL SX-class vessels** are the world's largest container ships. The first to be built, the *Shenzhen*, is 1,060 feet long and over 130 feet wide. The vessel was launched on April 30, 2003.

★ **Over the years**, container ships have been modified to better suit the products they carry. Some carry sophisticated refrigerated containers for transporting perishable commodities such as fish, meat, and fruit. These are called refrigerated ships, or "reefers."

★ **Reefers** contain heavily insulated compartments. These ships have several locker spaces that can carry different products at a variety of temperatures. The cargo is moved about on conveyor belts or by electric forklift trucks.

★ **Reefer equipment** has been modified to keep the goods they carry as fresh as possible. Most reefer containers have their own refrigeration units, which can be plugged into the ship's power source. If necessary, some reefers can even provide a humid environment for protecting sensitive products from dehydration.

Luxurious liners

★ **Ships in ancient times** were not only used to carry goods, but were also a popular mode of transportation for people. Until the invention of the airplane, ships were the only way that people could cross the seas to new lands.

★ **Ships that carry people** are called passenger ships. These can vary in size. Smaller vessels are used for short, coast-to-coast journeys, while large ships with lavish amenities, called cruise ships, are used for pleasure trips.

★ **Cruise ships** appeared only toward the latter half of the 20th century. Before that, intercontinental voyages were undertaken in large, motorized ships known as ocean liners.

★ **Ocean liners** thrived toward the end of 19th century, when millions of people each year were emigrating from Europe to the United States. Some of the most famous ocean liners were the *Titanic*, *Mauretania*, *Normandie*, and *Lusitania*.

▼ *The* Queen Mary *was 1,017 feet long. It was launched by the* Cunard *line to compete with France's* Normandie.

★ **The increased use** of ocean liners led to the establishment of several shipping companies. The better known of these included the White Star Line and the Cunard Line.

★ **The Cunard Line** is a British company that today owns the famous cruise ships *Queen Elizabeth 2* and *Queen Mary 2*. It was set up by Samuel Cunard, a Canadian shipping pioneer who, along with a few others, formed the British and North American Royal Mail Steam Packet Company.

★ **The first regular steamship** service between Europe and the United States was the Cunard Line. Two huge Cunard liners, *Mauretania* and *Lusitania*, were launched in 1906. They were both around 785 feet long. The latter was sunk by a German submarine in 1915.

★ **The Cunard liners** were not the fastest or the largest. In fact, the company's rivals, the White Star Line, owned the fastest ships of that time. However, Cunard ships were known for their safety—a feature that set the company apart.

★ **World War I** (1914–1918) severely disrupted the transatlantic service. Some liners were taken over and used to transport troops. After the war, the transatlantic services recovered and boomed.

★ **France launched the** *Normandie*, a liner famous for its luxury and modern art. The revival, however, did not last long. World War II (1939–1945) and the advent of jet airplanes in the 1950s effectively put an end to the transatlantic ocean liners.

The *Titanic*

⭐ **The *Titanic*** was the pride of the White Star Line, a British shipping company. Built in Belfast, Northern Ireland, U.K., the luxury ocean liner was one of the largest passenger steamships of the time.

⭐ **The ship** belonged to the company's Olympic-class liners. The others in this line were the *Olympic* and *Britannic*. The *Britannic* sank in 1916 after striking a mine laid by a German submarine in the Aegean Sea.

⭐ **Like all transatlantic liners**, it was meant to transport passengers between Europe and the United States. It was about 850 feet long and 92 feet wide.

⭐ **The ship had about 900** crew members and could carry over 3,000 passengers. Since the *Titanic* also carried mail, it was categorized as a Royal Mail Steamer, or RMS.

⭐ **The *Titanic*** was the ultimate name in luxury at the time. Its most striking feature, the grand staircase, was immortalized in James Cameron's epic film. The ship had 16 watertight compartments in its hull and was thought to be unsinkable.

⭐ **At noon on April 10, 1912**, the *Titanic* began her maiden voyage. She set sail from Southampton, England, U.K., toward New York. Among the passengers were several famous personalities, including the American businessmen Benjamin Guggenheim and John Jacob Astor IV, and the writers Jacque Futrelle and Francis Davis Millet.

⭐ **Four days later**, on April 14, the ship struck an iceberg off the coast of Newfoundland. It was almost midnight.

▲ *After its collision with an iceberg, the* Titanic *took only three minutes to break apart and start sinking.*

🟊 **The iceberg** ripped through the hull, causing the first six watertight compartments to flood. The ship broke in two and the bow sank almost immediately. It was followed by the stern, which hit the ocean bottom at high speed, severely damaging the hull.

🟊 **Another steamship**, the *Californian*, was anchored nearby. The crew members saw white rockets being fired from the *Titanic*, but failed to recognize these as distress signals. By the time the Cunard liner *Carpathia* came to the rescue, almost 1,500 passengers had died. Only 712 passengers survived.

Cruise ships

★ **By the end of the 1950s**, ocean liners were replaced by jet planes as a popular mode of transportation. More and more people chose to fly in order to save time. However, some still preferred the leisurely aspects of sailing the oceans.

★ **Pleasure voyages** aboard ships soon became popular, beginning a new era in cruising. Today, cruise ships are an integral part of the tourism industry.

★ **Like ocean liners**, modern cruise ships also boast lavish decor and comforts. Cruise ships, however, give more importance to amenities as compared to ocean liners, which put speed above all.

★ **Ocean liners** undertook long voyages across the Atlantic Ocean, and even traveled as far as South America and Asia. However, modern cruise ships mainly operate on shorter routes and make more stops.

★ **In addition to the crew**, these liners also have a separate hospitality staff. Some cruise ships have more staff than passengers in order to offer superior service.

★ **Until the 1980s**, cruise ships were not as huge as the ocean liners. Knut Kloster, the director of Norwegian Caribbean Lines, changed that when he bought one of the biggest ocean liners, the SS *France*, and renovated it. He converted it into a cruise ship and renamed it SS *Norway*.

⭐ **Soon large cruise vessels** became the norm. Today, most modern cruise ships are over 1,000 feet in length. The longest is the *Queen Mary 2*, at 1,132 feet.

⭐ **Today**, there are several shipping companies that offer cruise voyages. The best known include the Carnival Cruise Lines, Celebrity Cruises, the Cunard Line, Royal Caribbean International, and Holland America.

⭐ **The Caribbean Islands** and the Mediterranean region attract the most cruises. Some liners also offer trips to the icy waters of Antarctica.

▲ *Modern cruise ships are like floating hotels. They come complete with restaurants, bars, lounges, theaters, libraries, sport centers, miniature golf courses, swimming pools, clubs, shopping malls, and casinos.*

The queen of luxury

⭐ **One of the most famous** cruise liners today is the *Queen Mary 2*. It is the flagship of the Cunard Line and was built to replace the earlier Cunard flagship, *Queen Elizabeth 2*.

⭐ **Prior to the launch** of the *Queen Mary 2*, *Queen Elizabeth 2* was the largest cruise liner.

⭐ **The *Queen Mary 2*** was named after another Cunard liner, *Queen Mary*, which sailed the Atlantic Ocean from 1936 to 1967. The original *Queen Mary* now serves as a hotel in Long Beach, California.

▼ *Unlike its predecessors, the* Queen Mary 2 *is not a steamship. Instead, it has gas turbines and diesel generators that power its electric motors.*

★ **The *Queen Mary 2*** is around 110 feet longer than the original *Queen Mary*. At 1,132 feet, it is the longest cruise liner in the world.

★ **The ship was christened** by Queen Elizabeth II of the United Kingdom on January 8, 2004. It can carry over 2,600 passengers, and boasts one crew member for every two passengers.

★ **This grand liner** has 14 decks of sports facilities, five swimming pools, and ten restaurants. Apart from the usual amenities such as a library, theater, and Internet access, the ship also displays over 300 valuable works of art.

★ **One of the features** that sets the *Queen Mary 2* apart is its onboard planetarium, which at times serves as a cinema and a broadcasting studio.

★ **The liner** made its inaugural voyage from Southampton, England, to Fort Lauderdale, Florida, on January 12, 2004. It carried 2,620 passengers on this voyage.

★ **Apart from the transatlantic route**, the *Queen Mary 2* also undertakes cruises to almost every part of the world, including the Caribbean Islands, the Arctic regions, and exotic locations in the Mediterranean.

★ **During the Athens Olympics in 2004**, the *Queen Mary 2* docked at the port of Athens as a floating home to dignitaries and celebrities.

Ferries

⭐ **Ferries** usually have fixed routes, schedules, and destinations. They most commonly operate from towns and cities near rivers and seas, and are an important means of public transportation.

⭐ **They mainly run** across rivers or bays, or from one point in a harbor to another. Long-distance ferries connect coastal islands with each other, or with the mainland.

⭐ **The Staten Island Ferry** in New York Harbor is a famous harbor ferry. The best-known long-distance ferry operates in the English Channel, between Great Britain and the rest of Europe.

⭐ **Large ferries** also operate between Finland and Sweden. Some of these ferries carry hundreds of cars in their car decks. Others even transport railcars.

⭐ **When a ferry** makes several stops, it is called a waterbus. Such motorized vessels are common across the major water channels of Venice, Italy.

⭐ **Ferryboats dock** at a specially designed ferry slip. If the ferry transports vehicles, the slip usually has an adjustable ramp called an apron to facilitate loading and unloading.

⭐ **Many ferry services** in Europe use hydrofoils, which are boats with winglike foils mounted on struts below the hull. As the vessel picks up speed, the foils lift the hull out of the water. This ensures a speedy service.

★ **The Spirit of Tasmania** ferries form one of the best-known ferry services in the world. It carries passengers and vehicles across the Bass Strait between Tasmania and mainland Australia.

★ **The world's largest ferry** operations can be found in the Strait of Georgia in British Columbia, Canada, and Puget Sound in Washington State. Each operation comprises about 25 ferries.

▲ A ferry is a boat or ship that transports passengers over short distances. Some also carry vehicles and animals.

Fishing vessels

⭐ **People have used boats** for fishing since the beginning of civilization. Commercial fishing may be carried out by a single fisherman who takes his boat out to sea, or by huge fishing fleets.

⭐ **Fishermen** in some countries still go out to sea in small wooden boats to cast their nets and wait for the catch. However, traditional fishing boats and methods have given way to bigger, more advanced vessels and new techniques that produce a very large haul.

⭐ **There are three main** fishing vessels that can be found across the world. These are trawlers, seiners, and long-liners. All these vessels are more than 130 feet long.

▼ Trawlers have refrigeration facilities, allowing them to keep the catch fresh. Hence these vessels can also stay out at sea for several days.

- **Trawlers**, also known as "draggers," drag heavy nets, called trawls, across the seabed or through the water. These vessels are mainly used to catch shrimp, salmon, and other edible marine creatures.

- **Whereas earlier trawlers** had sails, the modern ones are powered by diesel. They are often large and can measure up to 400 feet in length.

DID YOU KNOW?

"Bycatch" is a term used to describe sea creatures that are not meant to be caught but are trapped inadvertently in fishing nets. Often the bycatch is not returned to the water despite the fact that it is unsuitable for commercial use.

- **Unlike trawls**, the mouths of seiner nets are closed before hauling them aboard. Seiners target fast-swimming fish like tuna and herring. The nets are allowed to float on the water to catch these fish.

- **Long-liners** do not use nets at all. Instead, they have long lines with numerous baited hooks along their length. These lines trail behind the ship, hooking tuna, cod, and even small sharks.

- **Other, less-common** fishing vessels include shrimp or lobster boats, head boats, and dive boats.

- **The sophistication** of modern fishing vessels has created its own problems. The use of modern equipment has increased the size of the catch, but not without greatly reducing the fish populations in many regions. Most countries now regulate hauls in order to prevent the decrease in fish populations.

Patrolling the seas

The oceans can be hostile at times. Danger can threaten those who venture into deep waters. Many countries spend a lot of money to ensure the safety of people sailing the oceans and visiting the beaches.

Authorities like coast guards, who keep a close watch on the activities on and off the coast, constantly patrol the open waters.

Coast guards help those in trouble at sea. They coordinate search-and-rescue missions, and are also responsible for protecting the coastal environment. They enforce maritime laws and are responsible for national security.

Coast guards have their own fleet of cars, boats, lifeboats, ships, helicopters, and planes. They use patrol boats to survey the surrounding waters of a coast and keep a vigil on all activities.

Floating hospitals, or "hospital ships," are large oceangoing vessels with medical staff and equipment. They are mainly used during a war.

Two of the largest hospital ships are the USNS *Mercy* and USNS *Comfort*, both of which are operated by the United States Navy. All modern hospital ships are protected under the laws of war and display the Red Cross symbols.

A lifeboat is an important rescue vessel. Lifeboats are of two kinds. One is carried by huge passenger ships, while others are launched from the shore.

Onboard lifeboats usually carry three days' supply of food and water, medical supplies, oars, and basic navigational equipment.

⭐ **Lifeboats** launched from the shore are called rescue lifeboats or rescue boats. Modern rescue boats are powered by diesel, while older ones, powered by sails, are also in use. All rescue boats have radios that help the crew locate ships and onboard lifeboats. They also carry first-aid equipment and food.

⭐ **The *Titanic* disaster** led to the formation of an ice patrol. The International Ice Patrol locates icebergs in the paths of ships and boats.

▼ *Coast guards are mainly devoted to maintaining maritime law and saving people who are in danger at sea. During wars, they are also responsible for harbor defense, port security, and coastal patrols.*

Tugs and icebreakers

⭐ **Tugs, or tugboats**, are small but extremely powerful motorized ships. They are mainly used to guide ships into the docks. They also tow defective ships, barges, and heavy equipment across open seas.

⭐ **Although they are small**, tugboats are incredibly strong. Modern tugs have diesel engines and can move at a reasonably good speed of 12 mph.

⭐ **Tugs are also used** to haul oil rigs to new locations. In addition, they can steer huge tankers in and out of oil ports.

⭐ **Tugboats** can be divided into two main groups: habor tugs and oceangoing tugs. Harbor tugs, or short-haul tugs, are used to move ships in the vicinity of the harbor.

▼ Tugboats are small, powerful boats used to guide ships to new locations.

▲ *Icebreakers have enough power to smash through thick ice in polar seas. They clear the way for following ships, which must keep up because the ice refreezes in a few hours.*

- **Oceangoing**, or long-haul, tugs are used to salvage ships from open seas and guide them to the dockyards for repair, or to tow floating docks and rigs to different locations.

- **Dredgers** are ships that collect sand and other sediments from the seabed. They are often used to deepen channels in harbors to prevent them from getting blocked.

- **Icebreakers** are tough, specialized vessels that are used to clear ice in rivers and seas in order to create a passage. They are very sturdy and usually quite heavy. They have an armored body to withstand shocks experienced during collisions with ice.

- **They ram into ice sheets**, or masses of hard ice, and shatter them. Sometimes they crack open an ice sheet by weighing it down with their sheer bulk.

- **Icebreakers** help clear the way so that ships can follow. They are also used for exploration in the polar regions.

341

Submersibles and tenders

⭐ **Specialized vessels** such as submersibles, tugboats, icebreakers, and dredgers often lend ships a helping hand and perform tasks that other ships are unable to perform.

⭐ **The submersible** is an underwater research vessel. It is primarily used to conduct underwater scientific research and for military and industrial purposes.

⭐ **Submersibles aid** in studies of undersea geological activity, marine life, and mineral deposits. They also help to check on oil rigs. Submersibles involved in research usually accompany a huge research vessel.

⭐ **Navies use** submersibles for a variety of tasks, including submarine rescue and repair, and mine detection.

⭐ **Wreck divers** use submersibles for salvage operations, such as recovering ships, planes, or valuable equipment that have sunk to the ocean depths.

⭐ **Pressurized submersibles** are designed to operate in very deep waters. They can withstand the high pressure near the seabed.

⭐ **The most sophisticated** of all submersibles are the remotely operated vehicles. These vessels do not need a pilot and are equipped with cameras and sensors.

⭐ **Tenders are ships or boats** that service other oceangoing vessels. There are various types of tenders, including ships' tenders and submarine tenders. Tenders of smaller boats are called dinghies.

★ **A ship's tender** helps transport people or supplies to and from the shore or another ship. A submarine tender is a ship that carries supplies like food, fuel, and other equipment to submarines. However, these are not very common today.

★ **Some modern cruise liners** have lifeboat tenders. In addition to serving as tenders, they also act as lifeboats. These vessels are bigger than normal lifeboats.

▼ The first range of submersibles appeared in the 1960s and 1970s. Today's craft are much smaller and more advanced but still work in the same way.

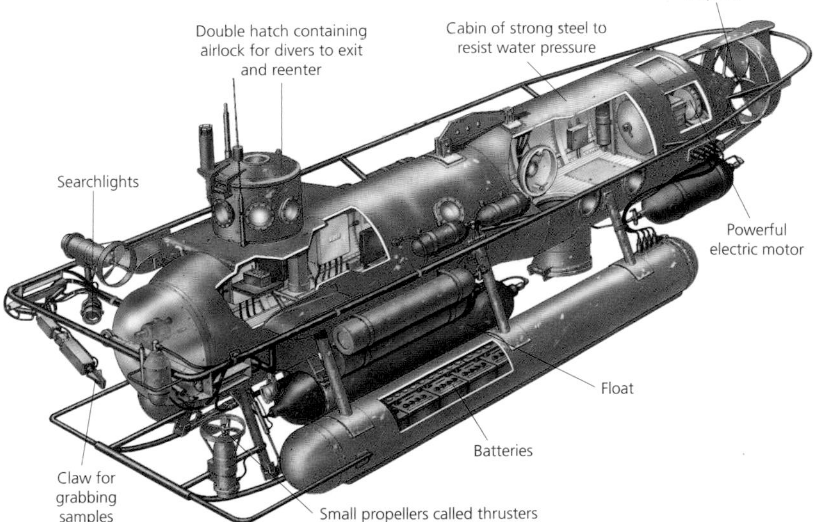

Propeller

Double hatch containing airlock for divers to exit and reenter

Cabin of strong steel to resist water pressure

Searchlights

Powerful electric motor

Float

Batteries

Claw for grabbing samples

Small propellers called thrusters to maneuver craft

Diving deep

⭐ **People crossed the oceans** to reach far-flung new lands. Soon, the same oceans started to draw our interest. Adventurers began exploring the ocean depths. This quest produced some great divers and explorers in the 20th century.

⭐ **Charles William Beebe** (1872–1962) was a famous deep-sea explorer. In 1934, he set a record by diving to a depth of over 3,000 feet off Nonsuch Island, Bermuda.

⭐ **The simple**, hollow, deep-sea diving vessel that Beebe used was called the bathysphere. It was invented by Otis Barton, a wealthy engineer, who accompanied Beebe on one of the most dangerous expeditions ever.

▼ *A scientist takes photographs of a great white shark.*

★ **Another renowned** deep-sea explorer is Dr. Robert Ballard. He is best known for discovering two of the most famous wrecks—the *Titanic* in 1985 and the *Bismarck* in 1989.

★ **With over 100** deep-sea expeditions to his name, Ballard has also written several books on his discoveries. His other findings include the *Yorktown*, the American aircraft carrier that was sunk in the Battle of Midway during World War II.

★ **Ballard** also led the team that discovered hydrothermal vents in the seafloor off the Galápagos Islands in 1977. His recent achievements include the discovery of two Phoenician ships off the Israeli coast. Dating back to about 750 BC, these are the oldest shipwrecks ever to be found.

★ **Marine biologist** Sylvia Earle is famous for her expeditions that focus on researching marine ecosystems. Earle holds the depth record for solo diving by a woman.

★ **Emile Gagnan** and Jacques Cousteau contributed to the field of deep-sea exploration through their invention, the Aqualung. This device helped divers stay underwater for several hours. It was successfully used during the removal of mines after World War II.

★ **Hans Hass** was a pioneer in scuba diving and underwater expeditions. His film, *Red Sea Adventure*, was judged the best underwater documentary at the Venice Film Festival in 1950.

★ **Undersea still photographers** and filmmakers such as David Doubilet, Stan Waterman, Michele Hall, and Howard Hall have also contributed to our knowledge of the ocean depths.

Diving through time

⭐ **The fascination** that humans have for the mysteries of the oceans is not new. History is full of stories regarding early attempts by ancient adventurers to become great underwater explorers.

⭐ **It is believed** that around the fifth century BC, a man named Scyllias, from the Greek city of Scione, saved the Greeks from Persian attack by diving beneath the sea and cutting off the anchors of the Persian ships.

⭐ **The history of diving** goes back to the time of Alexander the Great. The Greek philosopher Aristotle recorded in his writings that a diving bell was used during Alexander's reign.

⭐ **In the early days**, the diving bell was the most widely used piece of diving equipment. Its origins can be traced back to ancient times, when divers placed inverted buckets and cauldrons over their heads before going underwater.

DID YOU KNOW?
In his account of the Athenian attack on Syracuse, the Greek historian Thucydides recounts how soldiers fixed wooden poles underwater to block entry into the harbor. These unseen poles caused immense damage to Athenian ships.

⭐ **These inverted objects** trapped air inside them, allowing the diver to breathe. These devices gradually gave way to a more sophisticated bell-shaped wooden barrel that was placed over the diver's head.

⭐ **Air was passed** into the bell through tubes that went all the way up to the surface. Over the years the bell was enlarged to allow for more air.

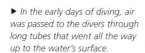

▶ In the early days of diving, air was passed to the divers through long tubes that went all the way up to the water's surface.

🌟 **A more advanced version** of the diving bell is still used today. Modern bells are made of steel and can withstand tremendous amounts of pressure.

🌟 **Divers in ancient Rome** were called *urinatores*, derived from the Latin word *urus*, meaning "leather bag." They got their name from the leather bag they carried while diving. These divers recovered treasures from sunken ships. They used heavy stones to help them dive to depths of about 100 feet.

🌟 **It is said** that around the first century BC, *urinatores* salvaged a cargo of amphorae, or ancient wine jars, from the ancient Roman merchant ship, *Madrague de Giens*.

🌟 **Divers** were also a major force in naval battles. According to historical accounts, Alexander the Great had to contend with *kalimboi*, or diving warriors, during the siege of Tyre in 332 BC.

347

Diving suits

🌟 **Diving suits** have seen many trends over the years. The earliest example is believed to have been made around the 15th century. The diver was restricted in how far down he could dive by his air tube, which went up to the surface of the water.

🌟 **It was only in the 18th century** that suits giving freedom of movement were first made. Klingert's diving suit, made around 1797, was one such suit. It was the first to be called a diving suit and comprised a coat and trousers made of waterproof leather.

🌟 **In 1819**, German inventor August Siebe made a heavy-footed diving suit using canvas and leather. The unique feature of this invention was a copper helmet that was supplied with air by a surface pump.

🌟 **Modern diving suits** can be broadly divided into soft and hard types. Soft diving suits are primarily used for scuba diving and other styles of diving. These suits protect the diver from low temperature but not high pressure.

🌟 **Hard diving suits** are more appropriate for deep-sea diving. They are armorlike suits that have pressure joints to protect the diver from the high pressure underwater.

🌟 **Soft diving suits** are of two kinds—wet and dry. Wet suits keep the body warm. They trap small amounts of water, which is then warmed by body heat. In turn, the warm layer of water keeps the diver warm.

🌟 **Divers entering colder waters**, such as the polar seas, wear dry suits. These are made of a waterproof material that keeps the diver completely dry. Divers wear special underclothes or use built-in electrical heating to keep warm.

▲ Divers control their breathing to make their
oxygen supply last as long as possible.

⭐ **Some suits** have a weight belt to help divers stay at the bottom. Headgear is equipped with visors and is made of the same material as the suit.

⭐ **Another invention** that revolutionized diving is the rebreather. Invented by Henry Fleuss, an English marine officer, in 1879, this portable air-supply system in the form of tanks freed divers from the constant dependence on air supplied from the surface. This was the first "self-contained underwater breathing apparatus," abbreviated to scuba.

⭐ **The invention** of the Aqualung by French divers Jacques Cousteau and Emile Gagnan in 1942 further popularized diving. A high-pressure cylinder, worn on the diver's back, is connected to the mouth with a hose that has a valve.

349

Reconstructing history

★ **Underwater archaeology**, also called marine archaeology, involves not only the discovery and study of sunken ships and planes, but also the unearthing of remains of ancient cities and ports that lie buried underwater.

★ **It is one of the most interesting** branches of undersea science. High-profile wreck discoveries, such as the *Titanic* and *Bismarck*, have only increased the popularity of this growing field.

★ **The discovery of cargo** from shipwrecks has provided a wealth of information regarding ancient trade and ways of life.

★ **Wrecks also** give an insight into the shipbuilding techniques of the past. The hull tells us how the ship was designed and built, while the sail and ropes reveal how the vessel was operated.

★ **A wreck's cargo** can provide information on whether the ship was a merchant ship, passenger liner, or warship.

◄ *Divers exploring a wreck. Modern technology helps us build a clear picture of how ships and boats were built and why they may have sunk.*

- **One of the best known wrecks** to be discovered is the Tudor warship *Mary Rose*, which sank in 1545. The pride of King Henry VIII, it was raised from the depths of the ocean and renovated lavishly for public viewing.

- **The *Mary Rose*** was raised in 1982, and the material from the ship offered a glimpse of domestic and military life during the Tudor reign.

DID YOU KNOW?

One story that has intrigued underwater archaeologists for years is that of Atlantis—the flourishing island that was believed to have sunk after a devastating earthquake. However, so far the search for Atlantis has been fruitless.

- **The discovery of a Bronze Age ship** in 1982 lent some credibility to stories about treasures in shipwrecks. This ship, which was discovered off Turkey, was found to have carried a tremendous amount of copper and tin ingots, indicating that it was probably a merchant ship.

- **Underwater archaeology** involves more than merely diving into the depths of the ocean and hunting for wrecks. Archaeologists spend an immense amount of time poring over history books and diaries of explorers to learn about various ships and where they sank.

- **Searching for lost cities** is another important aspect of marine archaeology. A thrilling discovery was the massive stone structures off Yonaguni Island in Japan, which may point to a civilization that existed 12,000 years ago but was buried beneath the waves.

Shipwrecks

🌟 **In modern times**, sophisticated navigational equipment has reduced the number of shipwrecks to a large extent. But until the 20th century, seafarers were completely dependent on dead reckoning and the magnetic compass.

🌟 **One of the best-known** shipwrecks is the *Titanic*. It sank after colliding with an iceberg. Today, with the aid of navigational instruments like GPS and radar, such disasters can be averted.

🌟 **Wars have claimed** several ships. Both naval and civilian vessels have been sunk by torpedoes fired from warships and submarines. In fact, the majority of the existing wrecks were a direct result of war. Most of them were sunk during the First and Second World Wars by German submarines.

🌟 **One of the famous casualties** of war was the *Lusitania*. This passenger liner belonged to the Cunard Line and was sunk during World War I by a torpedo from a German submarine off the southern coast of Ireland. Around 1,200 people were killed.

🌟 **On July 19, 1545**, the English Tudor warship *Mary Rose* sank unexpectedly during a battle with the French. The ship went down near Portsmouth, England, killing almost all its crew members.

🌟 **The actual reasons** behind the sinking of the *Mary Rose* continue to be a mystery. But it is believed that overloading and human error, not French cannons, may have sealed the ship's fate.

🌟 **The *Bismarck*,** the pride of the German navy during World War II, was responsible for several attacks on both merchant and naval vessels. The most noteworthy of these was the sinking of the British warship *Hood* in May 1941.

⭐ **The *Bismarck***, in turn, was sunk by British ships hungry for revenge. After a long battle, Germany's most dreaded weapon finally sank three days after the *Hood*, taking with it over 2,000 sailors. The remains of the *Bismarck* were discovered in 1989, off the coast of Ireland.

⭐ **The famous Argentine battleship** *Belgrano* became the first ship to be sunk by a nuclear-powered submarine during a conflict. The British submarine *Conqueror* sank the vessel during the Falklands War of 1982, killing over 300 people. The wreck of the *Belgrano* is yet to be discovered.

▼ Water pours into the hull as the Mary Rose heels over. At this point, there was so much water inside that sinking was unavoidable.

Raising the wreck

✦ **Raising a shipwreck** is challenging and involves a lot of risk. Wreck divers have to cope with low visibility, as well as with the discomforts of staying underwater for long periods.

✦ **A common risk** that divers face is getting trapped under hanging wreckage that gets dislodged.

✦ **Wreck diving** has developed over the years. Advances in the design of diving equipment and other inventions such as submersibles and remotely operated vehicles have made wreck diving safer than before.

✦ **A remotely operated vehicle**, or ROV, is an underwater robot equipped with cameras that is operated by people aboard a ship. The ROV is connected to the ship by cables that carry signals back and forth.

✦ **The extreme conditions** that prevail in the ocean depths have prevented researchers from conducting deeper explorations. However, it is now possible to reach these depths with submersibles.

✦ **The reflection** of underwater sound waves is used to detect objects in the sea. This method is known as sound navigation and ranging, abbreviated to sonar, and is one of the most important tools in undersea exploration.

DID YOU KNOW?

In 1989, Robert Ballard came up with an innovative method, called telepresence, which used advanced communication technology to transmit video images of wrecks across the world. This program was named the JASON Project.

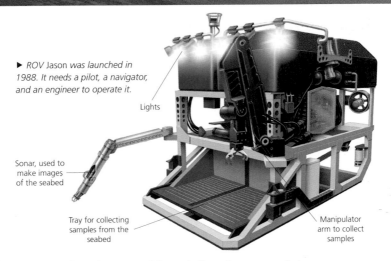

▶ ROV Jason was launched in 1988. It needs a pilot, a navigator, and an engineer to operate it.

Lights

Sonar, used to make images of the seabed

Tray for collecting samples from the seabed

Manipulator arm to collect samples

⭐ **Early wreck explorers** used diving bells and compressed air to go down into the water. But the pressure restricted their movements and research activity on the ocean floor.

⭐ **The revolution in wreck exploration** took place with the discovery of the *Titanic* in 1985. This was the first time that high-tech equipment was used to locate parts of the wreck.

⭐ **Robert Ballard**, the explorer who discovered the wreck of the *Titanic*, used an ROV sled, called the *Argo*, to explore the depths of the ocean. The *Argo* was equipped with night-vision cameras and other technology that supplied data through fiber-optic wires to the research vessel.

⭐ **After discovering** the *Titanic* in 1985, Ballard returned to the site a year later. This time he went underwater in a manned submersible named *Alvin*. A remotely operated vehicle, *Jason Junior*, accompanied *Alvin* to take pictures of the wreck.

355

Diving

⭐ **There are two kinds of diving**—recreational and professional. Recreational diving is a favorite pastime of tourists and amateur divers who like to explore the ocean floor for fun.

⭐ **Professional** divers are those who dive underwater for specific purposes, such as conducting scientific studies, repairing oil rigs, and retrieving wrecks or military equipment.

▼ *Today, diving has become one of the most popular water sports. People can explore an amazing underwater world and study marine life.*

- **Coral reefs** are ideal spots for amateur divers. The Caribbean is one of the most popular places for diving.

- **Snorkeling** is one of the oldest forms of recreational diving, and does not require any specialized gear. A swimsuit, a mask, flippers, and a snorkel (breathing tube) is the only equipment required.

- **Snorkelers swim** facedown on the surface of the water with their snorkels above the surface. This allows them to breathe while they observe life underwater.

- **While many children and adults** enjoy snorkeling, the more adventurous prefer scuba diving.

- **Scuba divers** wear a metal tank filled with compressed air on their back for breathing. The air pressure is controlled by a regulator. Air from the tank flows through a hose into the diver's mouth.

- **Scuba divers** also wear a heavy belt around their waist. This helps them to stay underwater. When they want to surface, they release the belt.

- **There are two kinds** of scuba equipment—open circuit and closed circuit. Both types consist of a tank filled with oxygen and connected to a diving regulator. In the open circuit, the exhaled gas is lost, while in the closed circuit the exhaled gas is recycled.

- **Emergency equipment** such as a knife, signaling instrument, and a light are essential for scuba divers. Some also carry a stun gun to protect themselves against sharks.

Living at sea

⭐ **Developers** are always thinking of new ways to make money from the popularity of islands and seas. Underwater hotels and artificial islands, such as the Jules' Undersea Lodge and the Palm Islands, are now capturing the imagination of people around the world.

⭐ **The Jules' Undersea Lodge** in Florida is the world's first underwater hotel. Named after the French science-fiction writer Jules Verne, it was a research laboratory that was converted into a hotel for divers.

⭐ **Visitors** have to dive more than 20 feet below the sea to enter the hotel through a "moon pool" entrance in the floor of the hotel.

⭐ **The Jules' Undersea Lodge** was first designed to be an underwater research laboratory called La Chalupa. Built in a mangrove lagoon, it was used to explore life on the continental shelf off the coast of Puerto Rico.

⭐ **The world's first** underwater luxury hotel is being built off the coast of Dubai, in the United Arab Emirates. The Hydropolis Hotel will be built on the floor of the Persian Gulf, 65 feet below the surface.

DID YOU KNOW?

The Jules' Undersea Lodge is filled with compressed air. This prevents the water from rising through the moon pool entrance and flooding the rooms.

⭐ **The hotel** will have three divisions. A land station will function as the reception area, while a connecting tunnel will transport guests from the land station into the depths of the ocean. A submarine complex will be the main hotel.

- **The Hydropolis** will also have two transparent domes that will hold an auditorium and a ballroom. The ballroom will be built above water, with a retractable roof.

- **The hotel** will be built of concrete, steel, and clear Plexiglas that can withstand high underwater pressures.

- **The Palm Islands** in Dubai, popularly referred to as "the Palm," are another oceanic wonder. They consist of two artificial islands in the shape of date palm trees.

- **Each island comprises** a trunk, a crown with 17 fronds, and a crescent-shaped island forming an arch around them. The Palm Islands will accommodate luxury hotels, villas, apartments, restaurants, and spas.

▼ The Palm Islands in Dubai are still under construction. When complete, they will increase Dubai's shoreline by 75 miles.

Rowing boats

⭐ **Since ancient times**, boats have been used for fun and sporting activities. Such boats include yachts, sailboats, canoes, powerboats, and rowing boats.

⭐ **Rowing boats** are moved with oars or paddles. They have been around for centuries. The rowboats used for sporting activities consist of a long, slender vessel called a shell. Although shells used to be made from wood, materials such as fiberglass and carbon fiber are more commonly used today.

▼ *Rowing can be categorized into sweeping and sculling. In the first type, each rower uses one oar, while in the latter each rower uses two oars.*

★ **Rowing** east to west across the Atlantic Ocean is tougher than rowing west to east because of ocean currents, and takes about twice as long.

★ **Rowing single-handed** across the Atlantic Ocean is a tough task. In 1969, an Irish rower managed to make the crossing from west to east in just 70 days.

★ **Some rowing boats** are steered by a coxswain, or cox, who sits in the stern, facing the crew. The cox steers the boat and encourages the rowers. Rowing boats that do not have a cox are called "coxless" or "straight."

★ **Kayaking and canoeing** have also gained a great deal of popularity in recent years. In both sports, rowers use paddles instead of oars. Unlike oars, paddles are not used in pairs.

★ **Both canoes and kayaks** are small vessels that are pointed at the ends. Canoes are mostly open-topped, while kayaks are completely covered, except for an opening for the rower to sit in.

★ **Canoes and kayaks** can be paddled by one or more persons. Kayaks have double-ended paddles, while canoes have paddles with single blades. Despite their differences, the word "canoe" is often used to describe both vessels.

★ **There are several sporting competitions** involving canoes and kayaks, including slalom canoeing, rodeo canoeing, and canoe polo.

Powered for fun

✴ **With the development of steam** and internal combustion engines in the 1800s, sails and oars became less common and soon motorboats were fashionable. Motorboats are fitted with inboard or outboard motors.

✴ **Some motorboats** use inboard motors, in which the engine is located within the hull. In outboard motorboats, the motor is attached to the stern of the boat and can be seen at one end.

✴ **Perhaps the most revolutionary** propulsion system for high speeds was the water-jet engine. In this system, water from under the boat is drawn into a pump jet and then expelled through an opening at the stern.

✴ **High-speed boats** are used in search, rescue, and salvage operations. They are also used for racing and leisure. Boats like hydroplanes and tunnel boats are especially popular among racing enthusiasts.

✴ **The streamlined hydroplanes** have projections called sponsons at the front. When a hydroplane picks up speed, it is lifted out of the water and supported by these sponsons.

✴ **The flat-bottomed tunnel boat** also has a pair of sponsons, one along each side of the hull. Like the hydroplane, the tunnel boat rises out of the water supported on its sponsons.

✴ **The runabout** is a high-speed motorboat that can hold around eight people. Runabouts can be used for racing, but they are more commonly used for fishing and water skiing.

✴ **Modern boats** are usually made of plastic and reinforced with fiberglass. These vessels are lightweight, fast, and easy to maneuver.

✴ **The most popular** kinds of powerboat racing include jet sprint and offshore powerboat racing. In jet sprint boat racing, boats powered by water-jet propulsion race in shallow watercourses with several sharp turns. Offshore powerboat racing takes place in the open seas.

▼ *Over 14 kinds of high-speed boats are currently used in powerboat racing.*

Surfing

Surfing involves riding the waves using a surfboard. Surfing is usually done where massive breaking waves are common.

Since the 1960s, the sport has grown in popularity. The dangers involved have only enhanced the excitement and glamour of this sport.

Surfers usually lie on their boards and paddle out to wait for a suitable wave. The idea is to ride a wave as soon as it starts to break.

There are several intricate movements and maneuvers in surfing. A surfer may ride the crest, or top, of a wave or its breaking curve.

The best surfers can perform maneuvers in the air. These moves, called aerials, were inspired by skateboarding and snowboarding. In a 360 aerial, a surfer does a 360-degree airborne spin.

Surfboards may be long or short. The longboards are over 8 feet in length, while shortboards are 6.5 feet or less. Both have small fins to help with stability and steering.

Long considered merely a local recreation, surfing is now a professional sport. Professional surfers generally use the shortboard.

Surfing is believed to have originated in Hawaii. Today, it is a highly popular activity worldwide, especially in Australia, South Africa, the United States, and Brazil.

In competitions, surfers are judged by the size of the waves and the distance they ride. Skills shown while performing maneuvers are also considered.

▶ Surfing requires great strength and agility and lots of practice. A good surfer has to be extremely fit and able to swim well.

Riding the waves

⭐ **Water skiing** is another popular water sport. In this, the skier is towed behind a motorboat at great speed. Water skiing can be enjoyed on large, relatively calm expanses of water such as rivers, lakes, and bays.

⭐ **The sport** was invented by an American teenager named Ralph Samuelson in 1922. Samuelson believed that it was possible to ski on water as on snow. He chose Lake Pepin in Lake City, Minnesota, for his first water-skiing attempt.

⭐ **A water-ski** run begins with the skier crouched low, holding the tow rope attached to the motorboat. Upon acceleration, the skier stands up straight and skims across the surface of the water.

⭐ **Water skis** are made of wood, plastic, or fiberglass. They are generally 5.5 feet long and 6 inches wide. Unlike snow skis, which have a rigid binding for the feet, water skis have rubber moldings.

⭐ **There are various categories** in water-skiing competitions. In the slalom event, the boat runs in a straight line while the skier has to zigzag on one ski around buoys. As the skiers successfully complete each run, the tow rope is shortened. The skier who completes the course using the shortest rope wins.

◀ Water skiing is now one of the most popular of all water sports.

▲ Jet Skis first went on sale in 1973. They can travel at nearly 60 mph.

Trick skiing is performed using either two short skis or a single ski. In this category, participants perform tricks, similar to those of gymnasts, while skiing. Skiers are judged by the difficulty of their tricks and performance.

In the jump event, a pair of long skis is used. Skiers achieve maximum speed before hitting a ramp floating in the water. They use the ramp to launch themselves into the air before falling back into the water again.

Show skiing involves elaborate preparations. With music and colorful costumes, skiers perform dance acts and ballets. Troupes also form complex human pyramids.

Jet Skis are also popular. These are motorized personal watercraft that look like motorcycles and travel at high speeds. Most Jet Skis can accommodate two or three people.

367

Index

Index

Entries in **bold** refer to main subject entries; entries in *italics* refer to illustrations.

Acknowledgments

All artwork from the Miles Kelly Artwork Bank

The publishers would like to thank the following sources
for the use of their photographs:

Front cover Reinhard Dirscherl/FLPA; Back cover (t) tubuceo/Shutterstock.com,
(c) Joanne Weston/Shutterstock.com, (b) JonMilnes/Shutterstock.com

Fotolia.com
21 koMa; 95 shardana; 214 Andrew Ferguson; 258 Antrey; 276–277 icholakov;
316 snowshill; 321 Ankya; 332 www.abidalphotos.com; 338 robdigphot;
341 BernardBreton; 359 Haider Yousuf; 367 razorconcept

All other photographs are from:
Corel, digitalSTOCK, digitalvision, iStockphoto.com, John Foxx,
PhotoAlto, PhotoDisc, PhotoEssentials, PhotoPro, Stockbyte

Every effort has been made to acknowledge the source and
copyright holder of each picture. Miles Kelly Publishing
apologizes for any unintentional errors or omissions.